ROOTED *in* PURPOSE

Overcoming Self-doubt and Pursuing Your Life's Calling

TRICIA ACHEATEL

HOKULEA PRESS ASHLAND, OREGON

*Rooted in Purpose: Overcoming Self-doubt and
Pursuing Your Life's Calling*
by Tricia Acheatel
© 2018 Tricia Acheatel. All rights reserved
www.rootedinpurpose.com
Published by Hokulea Press, Ashland, OR

Editing and Proofreading: Kendall Davis
Book design: Book Savvy Studio

ISBN: 978-0692077207
Published by Hokulea Press - First Edition published in 2018
Printed in the United States of America

DEDICATION

This book is dedicated to every woman who has ever felt less than enough. May you find peace within yourself and clarity about the unique gifts that only you can offer the world. May you believe in your power and act on your calling so that you can live the life of your dreams. I express deep gratitude to the friends and family who encouraged and supported me through this journey and the teachers who have been my guiding light through the manifestation of this work.

To be rooted means to be established, firmly and deeply. Purpose is the reason for which something or someone exists.

To be Rooted in Purpose is to be firmly and deeply established in the reason for your existence.

CONTENTS

PREFACE

Rooted in Purpose will walk you through a <u>step-by-step</u> program that shows you how to connect with your **true self** and create the life you were **born to live.**

This book is intended for any woman:

- Who is experiencing a **life transition** – the loss of an identity due to a change in employment, career, relationship, or health

- Who knows there must be **more to life** and feels a pull towards something but just cannot figure out what it is or how to do it

- Who is in **overwhelm**, being pulled in different directions with little time for self-care

- Who is unable to recognize accomplishments and in the face of success, **feels like a fraud**

- Who tends towards **perfectionism**

- Who feels "**not smart enough**"

- Who shoulders life **alone** and doesn't ask for help or support

- Who wants to feel courageous enough to **show up and be seen**

    Rooted in Purpose is a process of getting unstuck and finding self-confidence through understanding your unique gifts so that you have the courage and the power to launch your dreams and claim the life you want.

Are you **yearning** to make your mark and have an impact?

Are you trying to be everything for **everyone else**?

Do you feel you are born for **something more**?

Do you have a **business idea** you want to launch, a nonprofit you have been thinking of starting, a **book to write**, but you feel blocked and cannot move forward with the project?

The **Ten Practices** in the Book Will Teach You How To:

- Remember your **true nature**
- Match your **unique genius** to what the world needs
- Overcome **limiting beliefs** that are keeping you small
- Reconnect with your embodied and **powerful inner wisdom**
- Plan and implement a strategy for **your creative endeavor**
- Learn how to invite and **collaborate** with supporters
- Feel **more joy** and freedom

The profound and effective tools outlined in *Rooted in Purpose* will guide you from being a good girl to being the brave change maker that the world is waiting for. Learn how to be **deeply rooted in yourself**. This is the pathway to your right life and potential for true happiness.

I wrote *Rooted in Purpose* because over 30 years of teaching, coaching, and mentoring women, so many clients and students have come to me saying "I know there's something more for me but I cannot see the way forward." I have guided **hundreds of women** on this exhilarating journey to a **deeper sense of self and purpose**. More than ever before in history, it is time for women to step into leadership positions and be equal partners in the decision-making process.

Join me for **the most important work of your life.**

Introduction:
THE WORLD NEEDS YOUR GENIUS

You were born with potential. You were born with goodness and trust. You were born with ideals and dreams. You were born with greatness. You were born with wings. You are not meant for crawling, so don't. You have wings. Learn to use them and fly.

— Jalaluddin Mevlana Rumi

My attention drifts toward the sound of the fierce autumn wind outside my office window. I stop my work and watch as the rest of the leaves twist and turn in the blustering gusts. The sturdy pines, cedars, and spruce trees sway in the relentless rush of elemental force. The trees bend pliably yet remain solidly unmovable.

We live in times of great change, critical times. Now more than ever, we must grow roots that are strong and deep, and stand immovable in our truth. These tumultuous times are demanding us to develop the deep roots of our values with a commitment to the unique way we each are here to serve. If there was ever a moment in history to sift through whatever might hold us back so we can rise in truth and power, this is it. The world needs your unique inspiration, invention, and creation.

This book is for those women who feel called to something more and are seeking a guide that will lead them back to their Original Medicine. I refer to this term used by indigenous people to describe the invisible healing power that everyone is uniquely born with to help the world. Michael Meade refers to this as the Unique Genius. Gay Hendricks calls it our Zone of Genius. Others refer to this unique gift within each of us as a superpower, a unique ability or special gift. Our Original Medicine comes easily and naturally to us and it is how we excel at helping the people around us, which in turn brings us energy, satisfaction and joy. Our Original Medicine is an agreement that our soul makes upon entering the world and it becomes the thread of our destiny. The journey of following this thread involves a pilgrimage to the center of our self and then back out into the world. That is the journey of this book.

In reconnecting with one's Original Medicine and from that seed, forming a meaningful calling, a sense of greater purpose will awaken. This brings a sense of aliveness, passion and joy that fuels wellbeing and the drive to contribute to the current issues threatening our world.

Within these pages, you will find an offer of simplicity in the process of designing a life around an Original Medicine. Yes, we are in times of great change. The blessing of this is that anything is possible when we connect to the roots of ourselves and collaborate with each other interdependently. These are trying times, but they are also magical times of potential. Let us each offer our unique genius to the milieu of possible solutions. No one has your Original Medicine. It's yours and yours alone and has been with you since birth, forged and re-forged through the fires of your life. This isn't something you're supposed to do, or you should do, it is what you were born to do. Your calling is born from the infinite connection between who you uniquely are and the unique array of your life's joys and sorrows.

The principles outlined in this book are universally effective for anyone holding back but needing to develop or nourish the roots that will provide the strong foundation for pursuing a dream. Plant medicine allies are provided in each chapter as additional tools that you can use to foster a connection with the body, the Earth and to ease emotional and physical tension.

Now more than ever before, women must rise. For us to rise we must first address the current crisis that is unique to women. This universal issue must be resolved within ourselves, individually and collectively. The impact of this shift will be felt collectively and just might be the one issue that needs to be addressed before we can come to resolution on any other global issues. And it starts with you.

Many of the issues currently being fought for by women are economic justice issues such as earning a living wage, job discrimination, and pay equity. The recent viral social media hashtag #MeToo highlights and denounces the issues of sexual assault and harassment. Sex discrimination continues to be an issue in higher education and the work place. There is a gender imbalance in science, technology, engineering, mathematics, computing, and politics. Women take on more student debt than men do, but then pay back their loans more slowly because of the gender pay gap. Men still vastly outnumber women in leadership positions.

There have been many excellent books about how women aren't equally represented in leadership positions. These books are critical to our understanding of how it's time for women to rise and be equal to men. The statistics clearly demonstrate how women are under-represented in decision-making positions. According to the Center for American Progress, in May 2017, women represent 50.8 percent of the U.S. population and earn 60% of both undergraduate and master's degrees. 47 percent of all law degrees and 48 percent of all medical degrees are earned by women. Women account for 49 percent of the college-educated workforce. So clearly the issue is not one of education disparity.

Yet only 25 percent of senior level executive positions and only 6 percent of board seats are held by women. And the most glaring statistic-- only 6 percent of CEOs are women.

The same issue exists in politics. According to the Center for American Women and Politics, in 2017, women comprise only 19.6 percent of the seats in the

U.S. congress and 19.3 percent in the U.S. House of Representatives.

At the same time, we are dealing with issues that have affronted women for decades, from sexual violence and gender bias to reproductive rights. We are facing our biggest global crises, from climate change and the threat of nuclear war to the refugee issue. It is becoming clearer every day that the status quo isn't working. The time has come for women to rise, step into their power, launch their creative genius, and assume equal if not greater decision-making authority to men.

I recently organized a talk for Jean Houston to speak to a group of women at the American Association of University Women. In the brilliant words of Dr. Houston, "The most important change necessary is the rise of women as leaders in politics, science, education and in every aspect of healthy community building. Their courage, passion and service for not only social awareness, but for critical social change will set a new course of excellence for nations worldwide." Women's intelligence, wisdom, ability to collaborate, and their unique problem-solving skills and perspectives are critical now.

We have the right education, we know there's a need, so what's the issue?

Women are the ones holding themselves back from participating. Holding back their ideas, their contributions, their leadership and their talents. In her book Big

Magic, Elizabeth Gilbert says "Too many women still believe that they shouldn't put themselves out there at all until they are perfect and beyond criticism. While being far from perfect rarely stops men from participating in the global cultural conversation." Nothing is ever beyond criticism no matter how many hours or years you spend trying to make it so. We must learn to accept our own imperfections and our failures.

As difficult as this may be to hear, it is part of our genetic memory as women to be submissive and allow men to dominate. According to new insights in behavioral epigenetics, traumatic experiences in our past, or in our recent ancestors' past, leave molecular scars adhering to our DNA. The experiences of our grandmothers and great-grandmothers become a part of us, like a molecular residue holding fast to our genetic scaffolding. The DNA remains the same, but psychological and behavioral tendencies are inherited. So, as women, we have inherited the suppression of the generations of women that came before us.

Rachel Yehuda, Professor of Psychiatry and Neuroscience at Mt Sinai School of Medicine, has done extensive research on how the effects of stress and trauma can transmit biologically to the next generation. This means that we carry residue on our DNA of stress and trauma from previous generations. In other words, inherited family trauma shapes who we are. But does it have to? Zen Master Thích Nhất Hạnh discusses the alchemy of allowing ourselves to feel our feelings—especially painful ones—and the liberating effect not only on ourselves, but also on our parents and ancestors. Through looking inward, confronting our past and allowing the felt experience, he explains, we can release the painful contractions so that they will not be transmitted to our own children and grandchildren. It seems that getting quiet, being still and allowing ourselves to feel whatever emotion arises and whatever physical sensation appears ultimately creates a space where we can accept ourselves and release not only the places where we might be working against ourselves, but also our inner struggle, as well as our inherited genetic trauma.

The only way we will change the epigenetics of future generations of women, for our daughters, granddaughters and great-granddaughters is by changing how we experience our lives now.

What I have learned through working with women individually and in groups, is that women lack confidence and hold themselves back because of self-doubt. So why the lack of confidence?

What is confidence? Merriam-Webster defines confidence as "a feeling or consciousness of one's powers." Richard Petty, professor of psychology at Ohio State University has studied confidence for years. He says, "Confidence is the stuff that turns thoughts into action."

Over the last 27 years, my work has been centered around the development and mentoring of women through career transitions, striving for work promotions, launching and growing businesses, and struggling with their self-worth. I have observed clear and common patterns among women of all ages and across cultural diversities.

Women don't express their needs in relationships—they tend to assume that their husband, boss, child, or siblings know what they are feeling and what they want and need. Then when they don't get their needs met, they tend to feel resentful and unappreciated, even abandoned. Other patterns include:

- They pull back and shrink down inside to avoid conflict and keep the peace. This is a self-protective mechanism to distance ourselves from someone who consistently hurts or manipulates us. But repetitively over time, it means we neglect ourselves, which breaks us down.

- They compare themselves with other people to confirm the beliefs they have about not being good enough. Or they seek approval from an outside source for their worthiness. Either way, this is seeking a sense of self from external sources.

- They don't start things, even when they feel ardent about it. Or they try, fail and get set back to the point that they quit or even hide.

- They don't want to do anything if they aren't sure they can do it perfectly. Or they get blocked from even taking the first step towards an idea due to limiting beliefs about who they think they are or how they aren't smart enough.

- They don't trust their gut and intuition because they are disconnected from their bodies.

- They have lost track of who they are because they have spent most of their life pleasing everyone else.

- Lastly, they don't ask for help and support and try to shoulder everything alone.

Acting bolsters our belief in our capacity to succeed. Confidence is a belief in one's ability to succeed. This belief stimulates action. Yet if we don't act, then how will we ever build our confidence? Through trying, through success and even through failure, we build our confidence. So, it starts with trying. But trying at what? Where do we begin?

I feel the struggles of the women I work with, trying to do it all and do it all well, taking on way too much because it's hard to say "no." I see them not speaking up when they need to or avoiding conflict because someone's feelings might get hurt or not putting themselves out there from fear of being criticized or rejected. When we don't live in accordance with what we know to be true for us, we build walls around us, which incites a war inside of ourselves.

I remember on many occasions feeling the inner turmoil of that war inside myself. My family moved several times during my first 10 years of life, so I attended four different elementary schools. We ultimately landed on Maui where I was one of the few haoles (someone who isn't a native Hawaiian) in Kihei Elementary School. I was a round peg in a square hole and although this ended up being a gift, it was painfully difficult for a 10-year-old who just yearned to fit in. I spent a lot of time and energy trying to belong, which meant molding myself into something that would be accepted by the masses in my community. This was impossible as a pale-skinned, blond haired girl in a sea of dark-skinned kids. Regardless of how hard I tried to fit it, I just couldn't. I didn't get that it was because I looked different. I was ridiculed, excluded, and bullied. In my youthful naiveté, I assumed what most kids do, that there was something fundamentally wrong with me. I developed armor to protect myself, a coping mechanism common after being hurt or experiencing trauma. We adapt to survive and in doing so, form layers of protection around fractures, in my case the belief that the way I looked wasn't accept-able, just as a tree will "wall off" an injured and infected tissue and then grow new wood around the wound to create a protective boundary. I learned early on to hide inside myself which set me up for decades of avoiding conflict, not establishing clear boundaries for my own needs and shrinking my own power to keep the peace.

So begins the process of losing ourselves just a little bit more every day. To compensate for the inner discon-nect with our true selves, we pretend that we are happy, confident, and successful, betraying ourselves in the process. Belonging to our tribe becomes more important than belonging to ourselves.

When we live our lives from the social construct of being "good," fitting in and doing what we think we SHOULD do, we have put our true selves, the selves we were born to be, in a box, hidden away in the garage and collecting dust. We aren't giving ourselves to the world the way we were meant to. Bringing our vulnerable selves out, in all our pain, honesty, compassion and glory is what will change our own world first. Then we might have a chance of changing the world around us. We need to do this for ourselves first and foremost. We need to do this for our daughters and granddaughters. We need to do this for all the women in our ancestral lineage and for the millions of women today who don't have the privilege of using their voices. We need to do this for humanity.

Life struggle grows our strong roots. Developing a root system that is strong enough to support our potential for outward growth is the essential first step. My own journey of struggling to find my true self has developed a strong root system that supports action, regardless of fear. Despite fear. Because of fear. Taking courageous action, although it requires vulnerability develops the roots which nourish a strong and confident sense of self.

I have witnessed and shared the journey of so many women who feel stuck, lost, exhausted and even hopeless. We have become so good as women at doing everything that society associates with being successful and doing it all well, that we don't feel like we even know who we are anymore. And yet we sense that there is something more meaningful for us. The number one question I am asked is this: I've done so much work on myself and I have a good life, so why do I feel so lost? Women who have felt the pressure of all the demands on them, to do everything they're doing and do it all well, balancing the happiness of everyone else, often at the cost of their own. It's time for women to reconnect with their true nature, and to relentlessly and whole-heartedly create, regardless of believed imperfections and potential social perceptions. Or failures. Our work is to liberate ourselves from the societal myths that are blocking us from living our authenticity. The world is waiting.

You don't need to be better or work harder. You are already enough, exactly as you are. Learning to belong to ourselves develops the strong roots that will nourish our outward growth towards true joy.

Many of my clients have reached a quantum moment in their lives where they woke up to the knowing that something needed to shift because there was important work they needed to do. There was a shift from focusing on family, career, fitting in and attractiveness to seeking personal growth, a sense of self-esteem, being connected to something bigger, deep joy and forgiveness. This is the moment of the quest for more meaning. If you are at this crossroads, you are on the threshold of your life's calling.

The pathway to your empowerment is about

becoming more of who you already are. You are the only you. Never again will circumstances come together in exactly the same way. There never has been and never will be another you, ever. Take my hand and we will explore your true self. What is unique about you and what you want and need to bring to the world. May our journey together take you deep into the rich and nourishing soil of your magnificent being.

Chapter 1:
THE CALL

It may be that when we no longer know
what to do, we have come to our real work
and when we no longer know which way to go,
we have begun our real journey.

— Wendell Berry

From the beginning of life, we're programmed into a linear perception of how it's supposed to work. We learn to talk and walk, dress ourselves, behave in a socially acceptable manner, attend school, attend more school, set our life goals, get a job, buy a house, raise a family, retire, and enjoy life, until we die. By the time we reach adulthood, most of us feel that we must do certain things to succeed at life. But what about all the obstacles that we encounter along the way, the losses and challenges and heartaches? Where do they fit into this linear model? Isn't it more accurate that we usually have no idea what we are doing and whether we have chosen the right life for ourselves? The "midlife crisis" is often the moment when we find ourselves in an existential crisis, wondering how we got to this point, feeling unsatisfied, uninspired, and stuck.

Life Happens for Us, Not to Us

When I ask clients to tell me about the life experiences they feel have shaped them, I hear deeply moving stories. I hear about how they developed an ability to listen wholeheartedly and be the person that everyone comes to, to unload, because of growing up with an alcoholic parent. They tell me how they developed an ability to make people feel good because they were the victim of racism as a child, how they learned that they were a good mediator from listening to their parents fight every night, or how growing up in poverty was the catalyst for starting a food bank. Without exception, every time I ask someone this question, they describe how they developed a certain quality, a unique quality that others come to them for. What is interesting to me, is more often than not, they hadn't made the connection until I asked the question.

Every one of us is born with something for which our community seeks us out. Within us, our spirit has a unique quality that we are ordained to share with others. This quality becomes our unique offering to the world, and as life happens, it gets honed and sharpened and refined. By the losses, struggles, and heartbreaks, life continues to call us to our work, no matter what stage we are in, or our age.

How do we uncover this quality within ourselves, our unique genius? The first step is spotting the illusion that the only value by which we see ourselves is through what we do, our occupation. Then our work is to grasp the spiritual energy that is thriving in us, however buried under accumulated limiting beliefs. Part of the uncovering process is following your life thread to see how everything that life has offered up to you, the good, the bad and the ugly, has led you to this moment in time and shaped you into who you are. What you learned along the way was the refining process of your unique genius. This sacred gift is your true power.

- What are the life experiences, trials and losses that have shaped you?

- Did you develop a connection to a strength, a skill or a gift because of that experience?

- Do people recognize a certain quality in you and seek you out for that quality?

- How have you been valuing yourself through the lens of your occupation?

- Have you diminished your gift because you feel it isn't as valuable as another?

- How has a "flaw" turned out to be a gift for you? It might be the very thing that you have most been holding against yourself. Often the thing we interpret as our biggest flaw, is what's most right about us.

- Our breakdowns lead to our breakthroughs

Someone I worked with told me how she never believed she was smart enough to do much of anything. She was 47 years old and an attorney. For years, she had been feeling stuck and unhappy, in work that felt like a black hole. From the moment she was born, she was programmed to believe girls could never accomplish anything because they just aren't smart enough. Her brother was nurtured and groomed for greatness and no matter how hard she tried, how committed she was to getting good grades and excelling in school and work, she never received the praise that her brother got and that she yearned for.

She chose to go into law because becoming a doctor or lawyer was the surefire way to prove herself. She accepted that she was flawed and that she wasn't smart enough. This flaw became the driving force that led her towards law and eventually herself. After disbelieving this limiting thought, she could accept herself for the first time. She had the ability to see that she was a compassionate listener and passionate about helping foster youth. It became clear to her that life had provided the exact array of challenges she needed. Her choice to go into law gave her the skills to create the life work that allowed her to offer her gifts and make a difference in the world. She has created an advocacy nonprofit for foster teens who get lost in the system. The conditioning of her family of origin was the wounding, the flaw that she accepted as the truth, was the driving force for her to accomplish the very career that she needed as the foundation for her life's work. Her wounding led her to make choices in compensation, which ultimately shaped her calling.

One kind heart has so much power to change the world. We each have a vitally important way to serve.

The Complete Wipeout

What I have learned through my work is we get called to ourselves by being destroyed by life. I'll share a story with you of a woman who was going through what I fondly refer to as the "complete wipeout." See if this sounds familiar to you. In the past year, her life had been pulled out from underneath her, leaving her stranded and alone as a single mother. Devastated and yet forced to begin a new life, completely alone and frightened to the core. She was dealing with a complete betrayal. Her husband had left her for another woman and it blindsided her.

She was dealing with psychic despair. You know, the soul ripping, heart rending pain that takes you to your knees? When we experience a dramatic wounding, like the loss of life as we have known it from a divorce, or job loss or the loss of a loved one or the loss of an identity, we are brought to our knees. We are forced to leave our life smack-dab in the middle of it. We are forced to face the world and start anew, even though we are crippled with fear, feel entirely fragile, and utterly panicked.

Where does one even begin? The first step, the only step at that point, is to dissolve into tears and warm blankets. Cry buckets of tears and just feel it. Curl up in a cozy blanket and rest. We write pages upon pages about how we're feeling, pouring out all the despair and anger and feelings of betrayal and grief. Just getting it out and on to paper. When a complete wipeout has torn your life apart, it offers an opportunity to start fresh, reimagine yourself, your purpose and forge into that rebuilding.

Then one day, something else happens. Just when we feel like we have been brought to the end of our own limitations, deep inside we hear a voice that says, "No matter what, I can make it. Whatever is inside of me is stronger than whatever is out there to defeat me. I can do this. I surrender." The moment that voice kicks in, everything changes. This is the moment of The Call. This is the transformative potential of how the most painful moments in our life can usher in stunning new levels of experience.

The complete wipeout has dissolved everything you knew and relied on. This forces you to rely on your inner voice. "So, now that your life has been completely wiped out, here's what you need to do." Each major life event offers an opportunity to awaken to a deeper sense of our unique self.

I have also seen how the process of complete wipeout can happen little by little. We begin to lose our passion for the life we are living, bits at a time. Maybe your job isn't as fulfilling as it was. A relationship begins to feel like it's strangling you. We realize we have been in a holding pattern for so long that it become intolerable, to the point that we say, "I have to get out of here!"

No matter how your complete wipeout began, it ends up the same for all of us. When we get to the point when the psychic pain and loss has spent itself and the realization sparks that I CAN DO THIS, in that moment, we have connected to our deep inner wisdom and are now being directed from the inside. Inner wisdom is the physical sensations in the gut brain, the bundle of nerves in the belly. We give up needing to explain anything to anybody. What I have learned is that we have to get stripped down to nothingness to find our precious, raw, tender, authentic self.

The moment this voice kicks in, watch what happens. Ideas start popping up and dreams offer inspirations about what you could do that you have never considered. You begin to have thoughts like "How can I leave this position/career/salary and do work to help environmentalists?" Or "How can I go back to school and begin a medical profession after being a homemaker for the past 15 years?"

Just following my 21st birthday, my dad died suddenly in a scuba diving accident. I remember the sequence of events in mind as if it were a movie in slow motion. It was the end of my senior year of college. I was living in a big house with 4 other girls and it was a week before finals. Everyone was buried in research papers and flashcards. I was invited to go waterskiing with a group for the Memorial Day weekend. I begged one of my roommates to come with, but responsibly, she said she absolutely had to work on her senior thesis paper.

About an hour after we arrived at the lake, she pulled into the parking lot. I was so thrilled that she had changed her mind and decided to join us. I ran to greet her and immediately noticed that she was acting odd. I asked her if everything was okay and she assured me that it was. She joined us at the picnic table and we continued our light chatter. I couldn't help but notice that she remained quiet. Again, I asked her if everything was okay and she asked to speak to me in private. I thought "Oh no, what did I do?" She looked at me, paused and with clear anguish in her eyes, said "Your Dad died." I was incredulous. "Stop it!" I said, "Don't even kid about something like that!" Poor thing, I cannot imagine how hard it must have been for her to drive an hour down to the lake and be the bearer of such awful news. "I'm not kidding, your mom called." I drove home with her, still in denial, still believing that there must have been some mistake.

That loss derailed me for several years as I plummeted through life, recklessly running as fast and hard away from myself and the pain I was experiencing. Home was never the same for me after that. I distanced myself from the pain by avoiding home, my mom, and anything that might uncover the gut-wrenching emptiness. I made career choices that I might not have made and ended up in relationships that weren't the best. Hindsight is 20/20 as they say, however I can see now that it was the most pivotal moment of my life. Without that loss and the ensuing experiences that followed, I would not have the spiritual belief system that drives my core values and likely would not be writing this book today. This complete wipeout led me down a rugged and difficult rabbit hole until what I ended up finding, was myself. When we completely lose ourselves, we are given the opportunity to truly find out who we are. In the months following my dad's passing he gave me a glimpse of the medicine I had within and there could not have been a more precious gift than that.

Life Transitions and the Loss of Identity

Since before the common era, philosophers have been saying "The only thing that is constant is change." Change is the certainty of life. It seems like just when we have everything figured out and we are finally in the promised land of ease and happiness, circumstances force a transition we weren't expecting and don't want to make.

These changes are almost always triggered by some kind of loss, the loss of a loved one, a job, a relationship, a home, youth, health. Life-altering changes that shift our self-image and our imagination of the future. Although we don't have to welcome life's transitions, it is essential that we accept them. Allowing change without resistance makes us malleable to being shaped by it, however painful it might be. If we can accept that life is happening for us and forging us towards our calling, we can navigate the challenge with self-acceptance. Our work during transitions is to be as kind to ourselves as possible. Self-care is our priority during times of change and helps us develop sustainable ways to stand in our truth. We will explore self-care strategies in Chapter 6.

Feeling deep sadness, exhaustion and insecurity was not how I had anticipated feeling after selling my business several years ago. In fact, all I could imagine was how free I was going to feel. And yet, during those first months, there was nowhere I had to be, nothing to accomplish and no one expecting anything from me. Exactly the reason I thought I would feel free to do whatever I wanted, to finally have the time for me that I had always yearned for. Yet in reality, I felt completely lost.

Perhaps you have experienced something similar when you went through a divorce or made a career change or after your children left for college or you retired from your life's work. Even though we may choose to make a change, it doesn't mean we don't feel the effects of the loss of that structure.

The death of an identity is like the shedding of a mask, which exposes the soft, tender, vulnerable places and opens the heart in ways we couldn't have imagined without the loss.

The process of losing an ego identity, although excruciatingly painful, eventually leads to more peace, clarity and magic than would have been possible without the loss. There is an emotional and spiritual rebirth that takes place when we let go of an identity. This rebirth is essential to becoming who we are meant to be.

Any life transition means the loss of one thing to activate our move into what is next. That loss must be grieved, felt, experienced in order to let go of it and be fully heart-open to embrace what's next.

Moving through the waves of change develops a faith and trust that everything will be okay, that the universe will support and guide us. And yet when we are at our lowest of lows, trusting can be the hardest thing we will do. We want to feel better now. We search for a quick fix to feel better. Some way to not feel the gnawing fear, even terror that can be so overwhelming, it seems we will completely lose control.

My experience has been that losing control is exactly what I needed to do. To allow myself to be enveloped in uncertainty, to melt down into nothingness for a new version of me to emerge. If I fight and resist the pain of the loss, then I will get stuck there and I won't allow the light of my soul to write the story of my destiny. If I keep holding on to what my ego fears that it won't be or have anymore, I will be holding back the magic that is trying to be birthed.

If I allow, even though it feels paralyzingly scary, my heart to open, I can fall in love with myself. This cannot happen if I am holding on to something I think I can't live without. So, I am asking myself as often as necessary – Am I saying this/eating or drinking this/ avoiding this, so that I will feel better? Seeking to feel better is grabbing for a life ring. Allowing myself to sink into the abyss is trusting that I am going to be alright. By letting go I am allowing myself to be launched into a new experience of life with opportunities I could never have imagined. Opportunities that I wouldn't have seen because my eyes weren't focused.

I stand in a circle with all my former selves – I look around at the lost 21-year-old, the striving corporate executive, the wife, the mother of a child at home, the daughter, the seeker, the store owner, the child needing approval, the teen longing for acceptance, the friend, the listener, the healer—my heart is full to over-flowing with gratitude. I tell my beloved selves that I'm moving on. I weep not for what they've gone through, nor for the pain they have experienced, I weep in gratitude to them for who I am today. I am who I am because of those previous versions of myself. I have not lost them. They remain within me as the many facets of my love.

In *Finding Your Own North Star*, author Martha Beck reminds us that many cultures value the times in our lives when we lose one identity and move towards another. In many traditional world cultures one would leave the tribe and wander without knowing if they will survive to make it back, and in that place of not knowing, they encounter something profound. They return to the community changed with only fragments of their former selves remaining. This human metamorphosis is an essential part of our growth journey.

The work of our lives is the ever and constant evolving of ourselves by getting stripped of identities and for a time learning to somehow be okay with not knowing who we are or where we are. To be willing to exist in the threshold times where we have no idea who we will end up being when it's over and trusting that whatever lessons needed to be learned were learned, and if not, they'll come around again.

The Wendell Berry quote at the beginning of this chapter says, "When we no longer know which way to go, we have begun our real journey." No longer knowing which way to go and the pain of life transitions is typically linked to the loss of an identity. When a mother is going through the empty nest transition, she is grappling with the loss of her identity for 18 years as a mother. After divorce, the identity of being a wife is gone. After retirement, that loss of career identity can be exceptionally difficult. Losing an identity to which we have attached ourselves leaves an abyss and can result in low self-esteem, anxiety, even isolation.

Attaching ourselves to an external identity instead of to our true self, sets us up for the abyss that results from losing it. Clients don't generally seek my help when they are doing fine and feeling good. They reach out when they are going through a major life transition. We've all experienced the metamorphosis of change several times in life, moving from adolescent to adult, from being single to being married, becoming a parent, changing careers. How traumatic the experience is directly related to how attached we are to the lost identity and what we are telling ourselves about what it means to be who we are without it. If the identity was limiting you from doing to the work of your unique genius, losing it was essential to becoming who you are meant to be. Fight to keep the identity and we miss the opportunity to be formed. You most likely know someone who has opted for a rebound relationship after a break-up. Our awakening must come from whatever means are necessary.

Change in itself is transitory and leads to new solid ground. Until our roots find that ground, our work is to be here now with the experience of loss. Feel your way through it, allow the pain, fear, anxiety, grief—to just be. Talk about it, write about it. Stream of consciousness journaling is one of the best ways to process the intense emotions we may be experiencing and downloading our thoughts opens the ability to hear the subtle whisperings of our soul. Just don't resist it or try to control it. Trust that this is life forging you towards your future self.

Connecting and being aware of our physical body is vitally important to the process of feeling our way through a transition. Grounding into the body has the effect of settling the mind and allows us to process emotion through the body. One effective way to ground the body is by having contact with the Earth, also known as "earthing"—lying on the ground, walking bare foot, laying your hands on the ground. Rest there and feel the energy of the Earth seep into your body. Visualize yourself as a tree with roots reaching deep into the Earth. Breathe.

The Victim Trap

Beware of the victim trap. It can be very easy when we are in despair to default to victimhood. "Why me? Why did this have to happen to me??"

Why did it happen to you? Ultimately, it doesn't

matter because it did happen to you, and it's an experience that can and will form and shape you. This is the stuff that heroes are made of. For every challenging trial that you go through, you are developing the very strength you will need to do your work in the world. This is the honing of your craft.

A client with fibromyalgia I worked with years ago, through her own long trial, developed a depth of knowledge about how to ease the headaches, muscle pain, cognition issues, sleep disturbances and mood swings of this condition. She developed such a foundation of knowledge that she decided to help others with fibromyalgia. She now knows that it was her calling to go through her own hero's journey so that she would be able to help others. She has eased the pain of hundreds who are suffering from this debilitating condition through her practice and her writings. If she had gotten mired in the snare of believing that she didn't deserve this fate, which she easily could have, considering how debilitating it is to deal with fibromyalgia, she would never have been open to how the challenge was directing her to her unique way to serve.

Life is our greatest teacher, taking us down the winding paths of change and transformation and helping us gain a profound awareness of our gifts, and our potential to serve.

Tools & Exercises

Journaling

Journaling can be useful when we feel restless or uncomfortable in our current life situation, or when we are into a life transition. Through journaling, your subconscious mind can speak and explore, unhindered by mental resistance. Here are the steps to a rich and awareness-provoking journaling experience:

- Select a notebook that is strictly dedicated to your transition writing. Choose an inexpensive one that will allow you to feel free to write without concern about how messy it ends up being. What matters is brain dumping your thoughts on to paper.

- Write without any concern of what it might sound like to someone who reads it. This is for your eyes only. You are not trying to accomplish anything or do it right. There is no right or wrong so don't read what you wrote or edit anything.

- Just writing for 30 minutes every day is the key. Dedicate a protected alone time every day to write without concern for anything or anyone else. Feel free to sketch, doodle, paste in pictures or express yourself in whatever way your heart directs you.

As you write, insights may pop into your consciousness. Write them down. Write whatever comes to mind without needing there to be a specific flow. Months down the road, as you reread your journal you may learn something significant. You might notice repeating patterns or cycles. You might notice that you have developed a new awareness or made progress on stubborn issues. Journaling provides a higher-level perspective and fresh vantage point during times when we are stuck in the weeds and cannot see clearly. Journaling draws forth self-compassion and deep wisdom.

In *The Artist's Way*, Julia Cameron describes a journaling ritual she calls "the morning pages." She describes the process as a way of giving voice to a deeper knowing that lives within. Morning pages are three pages of longhand, stream of consciousness writing done upon waking each day. She reminds us not to over-think our writing. "They are about anything and everything that crosses your mind. Morning pages provoke, clarify, comfort, cajole, prioritize and synchronize the day at hand."

Journaling can be a farewell to life, as you knew it and an introduction to the unfolding future. Grief, anger, fear and feelings of helplessness – expressing these accumulated emotions creates clarity. New possibilities arise and in the process of wholehearted expression through journaling we can unleash gratitude, joy, and a lightness of spirit.

If you are in the midst of an ending or transition in your life, know that the intensity you are feeling is a transformative fire that, in the end, is bringing you home to your immutable, radiant self. The endings we face may be unwanted and difficult, yet they can lead us to a deeper connection with life. Instead of scurrying around trying to get out of this transition as fast as you possibly can, try exploring its possibilities. Try to relax into the not-doing and try not-thinking. Allow the new self that is forming to emerge.

If you are navigating your own complete wipeout or life transition, you are right where you need to be. Continue your writing and self-care.

As I read back over my daily entries over a six-month span of morning pages, I can see a forming of and recovering of my personal identity. What emerges from my musings is an increasing sense of safety in expressing my deepest fears and gradual unfolding of a sense of strength. My entries reveal a compassion that my adult self sends to the sad and lonely 10-year-old who needed to hear that everything was going to be okay. An early entry from my morning pages:

"I felt so lost most of time and spent endless afternoons alone riding my bike. Thank God for Kui (my dog) because she saved me and became my best friend. I remember that day as if it was just last year—riding my bike down Kihei Road and seeing the sign for puppies and then going home and asking if I could get a puppy and Mom saying yes. Riding back and putting Kui in the basket on my bike to bring her home. Kui, thank you for being there for me. Poor baby 10-year-old girl. Why couldn't anyone see how sad you were?

Like you didn't matter to anyone. What was it that you wanted to hear? 'It must be hard to feel so alone. You are beautiful, you are loved, it will all be okay. I'm here for you. Let me hold you darling.' Comfort and acceptance and love. That poor sweet girl in so much pain."

The process of writing to my 10-year-old self gave her the love that she needed. That girl is still inside of me. I can be the one now, who gives her the love and compassion. As adults, we can offer care and compassion to the parts of us that are still hurting. Journaling and morning pages give us a safe place to uncover the tender, scared, ashamed parts of us that are crying out for love.

As a practitioner of western herbal medicine, I offer suggestions of plant allies to assist in nourishing your body, nurturing your soul, connecting with the Earth and recalling yourself as a healer.

Women have always been healers. I have found through my work with clients and students of plant medicine over the past several decades that the simple act of intentionally connecting with a plant, the beauty of making tea and the sacred act of drinking it, is the single most effective way to connect with our ancestral feminine lineage and the Earth. Waking up our genetic memory reignites the ancient healer in each of us. This awakening connects us to the greater connectivity of the Universe as well as to our most elemental power.

One powerful way to ground the body is through plant medicine.

Milky Oats

Milky Oats is one of my favorite plants for nourishing and calming the nervous system, relieving stress and centering both the physical and emotional bodies. It is restorative and nutritive tonic. Milky oats are the oat tops harvested when they are in their milky stage. Milky oat tops make a delicious herbal infusion or tea.

Avena sativa, Oats

The grieving process is a rite of passage in which the seeds of the future are planted in the soil of our being and watered by our tears.

Chapter 2:
THE FRACTURE

You may encounter many defeats, but you must
not be defeated. In fact, it may be necessary to
encounter the defeats, so you can know who
you are, what you can rise from, how you can
still come out of it.

— Maya Angelou

The Journey Ahead

This book will take you through a journey of self-discovery. Through twists and turns, occasional setbacks and defeats, yet persistently towards the unencumbered light that has always been there to guide you, is still there, beckoning a reunion. Let's explore the steps of this passage from Good Girl to a Badass who is living in her truth and changing the world with her presence.

Along the way, we will be learning tools that will guide your journey, just as Dorothy encountered demons and challenges, she also received guidance and gifts, and so will you.

- **The Fracture.** This is where the root cause of where the self-doubt and shame began. It's time to grow up, get out of the past and into who you are now. We will explore how **somewhere along the line, most of us received a wound or fracture that disconnected us from our true nature. What was the message you received? When did you stop being yourself, so you would belong?** Whose voice is it that you're using against yourself?

- **The Good Girl.** How does being a Good Girl block access to your inner wisdom? We need to learn how to live in integrity with ourselves. This means doing what WE want and need to do, rather than what we believe we should do. To follow and stay true to this guidance, it is essential that we develop clear boundaries. This means speaking our truth and saying "no" when we need to rather than saying "yes" so that we don't ruffle feathers, hurt feelings or appear unhelpful. Having strong boundaries also means choosing to clear up conflicts instead of avoiding them.

- **New Beliefs.** Learning the process of identifying and questioning beliefs that are sucking our power and keeping us small is the most integral tool that I use with women who want to pursue a dream. This is about breaking free of the thoughts that something is wrong with you. Identifying the self-berating things you say to yourself. We will explore neuroplasticity and how our thoughts create our experience of life.

- **Original Medicine.** Your Original Medicine or unique genius is the gift you must offer the world. We will go back through your life experiences and explore the ways that you show up to serve. This unique quality that you and you alone have is what a life calling is built around. It is the foundation of who you are and were born to be.

- **Hold Fast to Your Thread.** Our bodies are the loud speakers of our souls, we need only to learn how to listen to the guidance that is there. We will learn how to use body wisdom to guide right action and direct our plan forward. Put simply, how to listen to your gut. At times, this might mean choosing to do the courageous thing that feels scary over avoiding the discomfort of how it feels. Feeling fear isn't necessarily bad and can mean we are doing something important. We will explore how to break free of that armor that may be protecting yet impeding you. Then how to remember to live an embodied life so that you can dream your ideal life into real.

- **Your Roots in the Ground.** This is about becoming the one you've been waiting for by taking real action towards the life you want to manifest. This involves making self-care a priority so that you have the bandwidth to accomplish what you set out to do. We will learn how to lay out a timeline and create a plan for the first steps for you to take to launch your dream. Developing your next steps with clarity, purpose and direction, with the knowledge that failures are opportunities, not proof of your unworthiness.

- **The Universe Conspires.** This is about following your bliss. But not alone. Learning how to come out of hiding, how to get vulnerable and ask for help, both visible and invisible. And how to surrender and allow divine grace to support your right life. Remember those boundaries? They will come in handy when you will inevitably face criticism and rejection. To do our work in the world we must master resilience against what people might say. I want you to develop a trust in yourself and faith in the outcome. I believe in you. Now it's time for you to believe in you.

Self-Sabotage

We all get in our own way. Life provides certain opportunities and choices, yet we allow ourselves to receive, achieve, or enjoy such opportunities only to the extent that we believe ourselves deserving or worthy of them. Low self-worth is the primary cause of self-sabotage. Every one of us can look back and remember a time when the universe presented an opportunity, opened a door to more success, more love, more happiness—and yet we turned it down. We allow this invitation to pass us by because we don't believe enough in ourselves to accept the offering. Then we look back on our lives from where we stand in the present, often with regret and see how we could have made different choices.

The past is over. It can only provide insight into how we might have been limiting our greatness then, and how we may be doing the same now. Why weren't you willing to step into more greatness at that time? Why weren't you feeling worthy of more happiness, more success, more love? How are you limiting yourself now from being as bright and beautiful and big as you can be?

You were born for greatness. You were born with unique and beautiful gifts to offer the world. The universe is a creativity machine that is constantly looking for who is ready. We need only be awake enough to see the open door. Are you showing up to be of service to the world? Or are you shrinking back and staying small because it feels safe, like a familiar habit?

There are various ways that this might look.

- You try every diet that you come across and they work for a while but ultimately stop working which makes you feel even worse because you failed yet again at losing weight. Is there a belief from the past that you are a fat, unattractive, unlovable person because you were a chubby kid and were ridiculed for it?

- A friend or colleague introduces you to a potential romantic interest. You try going out on a date or two but decide to discontinue the association because you feel uncomfortable every time you're with him, you're just not ready, or he just isn't what you are looking for. Was there a message that you internalized from the past that you are just not good enough and therefore not worthy of love?

- You feel unsatisfied or even miserable in your current job, but the idea of changing careers feels too daunting. Much easier to just stay where you are instead of taking the risk at trying something new. Is what is really holding you back, that you feel like a failure and don't deserve to be happy anyway?

No matter what your situation is, if it sounds anything like these common examples, then there is something in you that believes you're not good enough. You keep telling yourself that same old story and it keeps you small. Staying small is the ego mind keeping us from being our greatest selves. Why is the ego mind so resistant to you standing in your full light? Why is the ego intent on you not being that big? Because being in your fullest, most beautiful greatness is ego-less and the ego needs you to need it!

You must clear up the past—despair will continue until YOU change, until you awaken. Opportunities will present themselves and you won't be able to see them.

What does it mean to awaken? Life presents opportunities, yet we cannot see them, or we deny our readiness for them because we are still holding pain from the past. Our beliefs created from past experience are blocking us from seeing the opportunities for more love, more success, more happiness. Waking up means clearing the windshield of dirty past pain so that we can see all the beauty and blessings within and around us. The more abundance that we acknowledge, the more abundance shows up for us. This is the benevolence of our universe.

To clean the glass of dirty pain, we must question

every thought that causes us suffering. Trace it back to where it might be coming from in your past. Self-limiting thoughts are the stories we tell and retell in our heads about a circumstance in the past, reliving it over and over and over, each time believing the lie that we aren't loveable, or smart enough, or thin enough, or good enough. It's time to wake up. Forgive whoever was involved, but mostly forgive yourself.

Tune into your body's wisdom. If the story is causing you pain, then it is not true. Question and disbelieve any thought or story that is causing you pain, emotional or physical. Come up with as many reasons as you can think of to prove to the inner critics in your mind just how untrue that old story is. First notice the pain, then identify the thought you had or the story you were telling yourself just before the painful sensation occurred. Write it down. Ask yourself if it's true. Write down as many examples that you can think of for why it isn't true, right now, in this moment.

And meditate. Meditation is the easiest and most effective way to get out of your thoughts and get in touch with your essential self, the beautiful radiant light that is you and is nothing less than perfect.

These words from *A Course in Miracles*: "The past is over, it can touch me not." We bring the past as baggage into all our relationships, experiences and business endeavors. What we need to learn is how to walk forward courageously into life, free of the past. This is how the past is no longer the glass through which we look at our lives. The past must be forgiven to be gone. Every time you beat yourself up for something in the past, then you are stuck there, not moving forward.

If you are thinking—I wish something good would happen to me! Then you need to hone yourself, prepare yourself so that when it comes, you are ready. You can see it in front of you and you are able to accept the invitation. In this way, you will greet the future with the most self-loving, self-accepting voice that you can.

This is the journey we will embark on together. Let's first explore the source of painful beliefs.

The Fracture

It is common for our emotional health to get damaged during childhood. Somewhere along the line, many of us have received an emotional wounding as children that disconnects us from who we are. A painful experience in childhood can shape our adult personality and our strategies for how we show up. This experience often shapes how we view the world and often hasn't been healed, even in adulthood. This wounding or fracture causes us to armor up in self-protection which can hinder our progress in life and block us from connecting with others as well as with ourselves. Childhood fractures are often centered around shame, the painful experience of believing that we are flawed and therefore unworthy of love. According to Lise Borbeau, author of *Heal Your Wounds and Find Your True Self*, there are five common types of wounding. These five types of wounding can show up in adults as fear of abandonment or fear of being alone; fear of rejection which can prevent us from accepting our own thoughts, feelings and perceptions; humiliation and fear of disapproval or criticism from others; betrayal or fear of trusting others; and injustice, which leads to feelings of powerlessness.

In my work with women, I typically see in equal measure the fear of rejection and the fear of humiliation as the most common causes of low self-esteem. Betrayal or fear of trusting others also shows up as a cause of perfectionism, not trusting anyone else to do the job "right."

Sadly, many women tell me how as children, they were told they were stupid, bad, overweight, not smart enough, high maintenance, needy, emotional, ridiculous, nonsensical, exhausting, selfish, spoiled, disappointing, and heard things like "why can't you be more like your brother?" It's not hard to see how adult women might have internalized any of these messages and are now overcompensating to prove to the world that it isn't true. What happened to the bright and shiny little girl that was bursting with eager anticipation about what life had to offer? Feeling flawed creates a feeling of being unlovable.

Without a tribe to belong to as a 10-year-old, I spent a lot of time alone, riding my bike all over the mudflats of Kihei. My bike delivered me into a feeling of freedom and still does. Every morning before school, at sunrise, I ran for miles down the beach in front of our house. My parents, although they were doing their best, didn't notice how much pain I was in. Or they did, and because they were uncomfortable with my awkward loneliness, tried to turn me into a more acceptable version of myself. What I needed was to be told that I was good enough. That I was loved exactly as I was. To have someone hold me and tell me it would all be okay, that they were there for me as my biggest supporters. As parents will do, my mom criticized me in the hopes that it would force me to be a different or better version of myself so that I would be happy and be acceptable so she wouldn't have to worry about me. We want our children to be happy and it's hard when we see them in pain. Perhaps my mom's discomfort centered around her own feelings of inadequacy as a parent.

When I was 15 and a sophomore in high school, I had a profound experience that was to be my first Call. I was so highly tuned to the environment around me, the gift of spending time alone in communion with the land and the ocean where we lived. I sat bolt upright in bed in the middle of the night, acutely aware that something was wrong on the beach. I ran down to the beach and found an entire pod of dolphins had beached themselves in front of our house. I spent five hours with them, pouring water on their skin so it wouldn't dry out and as the tide started coming in, helping them back into the water. By the time the sky started getting lighter and the sun popped up above the horizon, all but three of the dolphins had swum out beyond the reef to deeper waters. Over the next two hours, the three remaining dolphins stayed with me, what felt like a conscious choice for them. I can still remember their love and gratitude as it filled my heart. This was my first experience of acceptance.

At the time, I did not understand that my life was forever changed by that experience. A part of me that I didn't realize was there, woke up. I had new eyes. I know now that I would not have had the awareness and sensitivity to feel what was happening with the dolphins, had I not been developing the depth of relationship with myself and other living beings around me all those years. That level of deep connection with an animal as intelligent as I could feel the dolphins were, confirmed my worth. The path to that experience couldn't have been more perfectly laid out for me.

By the time I was starting college, I had mostly forgotten my prior shame of not fitting in. I had a new sense of myself, I knew there was a deeper purpose for my existence, although it was just a whisper. I still had my protective armor; I was still keeping myself safe from not belonging, or so I believed. What I didn't realize at the time was I had picked up where the bullies left off. A steady barrage of mean self-attacks ran through my brain every day. Nobody knew. I didn't even know for many years. I began striving in many ways to prove my worth. In Chapter 3, I'll explain how striving is a classic survival strategy for women. At the time, I had no idea that this wasn't going to bring me more happiness or belonging. I learned that much later.

The dolphins had ignited a glowing ember in me, but my armor blocked me from fanning the ember into a flame. Until my armor got blown to bits, when my Dad died suddenly, just a few years later. When we understand where our fracture began and how we began to protect and adapt ourselves to compensate so that we would be worthier of love and belonging, we can get a sense for how we began to lose our true selves. In the next chapter, we will explore the most common ways that women compensate.

In my first ten years of clinical herbal practice, I documented an observation about healing, a common pattern that presented with many of my clients. I specialized in women's health and saw clients with a myriad of presenting issues, from hormonal imbalances to digestive disorders and auto-immune disorders. After making nutritional and lifestyle changes and taking their herbal formulas for a period, most everyone would get better within a few months, even be symptom-free. Herbal medicine is extremely effective for chronic conditions. What I didn't expect was that a year or two or three later, the presenting symptoms and condition would often have returned. When I reviewed the charts of the clients who had conditions that had returned, they all shared a similar experience of childhood wounding that hadn't been healed. I became fascinated with the connection between and interdependence of the physical, emotional and spiritual bodies.

When something painful happens, particularly in

childhood, we deal with it the best we know how with the resources we have in that moment. We carry on. This is how we cope and learn to protect ourselves. We tend to store life experiences in our bodies and when an experience is particularly painful, our mind avoids going there with our attention. Trauma can be any stressful experience in which we didn't have the emotional resources to deal with it at the time. The brain considers stored life experiences to be a danger which can activate fear. This is a mind-body disconnect. Disassociation from the body is a natural survival technique. We can relearn the skill of staying with the body rather than leaving it when we experience discomfort. In *Trauma Releasing Exercises*, David Berceli writes, "Just as this body/mind continuum is a natural mechanism that has protected humans during their evolution, these same natural mechanisms continue to restore us to health."

Tools and Exercises

Mind-Body Connection

Creating mind-body awareness allows us to become the compassionate observer of the mind, body, and emotions. This isn't about needing to fix anything, we are simply seeking to connect and learn. Several times a day, take a few minutes of quiet noticing of yourself. You can set a timer to do this three times a day. This self-awareness is helpful at any time but particularly when we notice a shift in our mood. The benefits of improved mind-body connection include stress relief, less anxiety, pain relief, increased energy, improved sleep, weight loss, enhanced connection with intuition and creativity, alignment with the soul's purpose.

To experience ourselves fully, we must allow all that is present to be experienced and to do this we must stay physically present in our bodies. We must be true to every part of us—the parts that we no longer need, yet which have brought us to this point and the part of us that is forming us towards what is to come. There is always something dissolving in each of us—relationships, health, youth, career identities, roles as children, as parents. When we run away from, avoid or resist our experience, including the sensation of emotion in our bodies, we force ourselves into helplessness and disorientation, shame and terror.

Take three breaths and ground your attention into your body. Feel your back, bum, and your feet on the ground. Sense roots going from your feet into the Earth. Notice that you are physically safe, right here, right now. Take one big breath in through your nose and slowly and audibly exhale through your mouth. You can hum or sigh, but really hear yourself exhale.

Body Awareness

Do a scan of your body. Notice any pain, agitation, tension, relaxation in your body and where it is. Starting with your toes and slowly moving up, become aware of the different parts of your body. Ask yourself what body sensations you are feeling, and where you feel them. There are no right or wrong sensations, there's nothing to fix, it's all just information. You're just gathering data. Are there any parts of your body that feel numb or frozen? Feel your big toe, rub your hands together and place them on that part.

Emotional Awareness

Sense how you are feeling—tired, sad, angry, anxious, scared, frustrated, joy, peace, excitement. What emotion are you feeling right now? Become aware of the subtle energy of the emotion you may be feeling right now and the physical sensations that it might be connected to. For a few moments, be willing to feel discomfort. Remember, there is not right or wrong here. Discomfort is not a negative thing, it is just information. Your mind might be saying "I don't want to feel this!" Tell yourself it's okay and stay with the sensation. Allow the emotional energy to move through your body without judging it or labeling it as something you shouldn't feel, or as bad or good. Just observe and experience whatever emotion arises. If it begins to get unbearable, try rubbing your feet together. Let your breath flow and notice if you are holding your breath and if so, let it move again.

Mind Awareness

Becoming aware of your thinking requires you to first notice your body and emotions because the mind tends to suppress emotion to avoid potential pain. We tell ourselves a story to avoid the truth and the possible pain that might come from it. To live an authentic life, we must dwell in truth. Notice what you are thinking. "What is my mind doing right now?" Notice any thoughts or anything you might be obsessing about, ruminating on, or overanalyzing. Any ways that you might be planning, arranging, worrying. Our logical and mental processing is one of our strengths as human beings, but it is only one of them and the one we rely on most heavily.

When you have time, grab your journal and jot down the things you notice, insights, observations or revelations. Parts of your body that felt numb or frozen may be stored painful experiences. Offer those parts love and compassion. Physical and emotional discomfort both carry messages for our growth and understanding. When we allow ourselves to hear them, the discomfort from them moves through us and the energy of the emotion can leave our body. When we suppress, ignore or avoid discomfort, the flow of energy is blocked which can lead to greater discomfort or physical pain, and more tension. Allowing our emotions to flow through us, and allowing our bodies to metabolize emotional pain creates the opportunity for discomfort to inform us. The most important thing we can do to maintain a mind-body connection is experience and allow our emotions. Watch the mind and allow the emotion to flow.

Ponder this. As you were noticing your body, mind and emotions, who was doing that observing? This is the larger us that we can learn to tap into. This is our wise self, our universal self, our essential self. Developing this kind of mind-emotion-body awareness is how we can clearly hear our intuitive guidance. This inner guidance is the strength that I invite you to welcome and develop. We are not our mind, our body, or our emotions, we are the awareness.

Our wise self can ask our discomfort for information, "How are you here to help me?" Inner wisdom comes from the body, not the mind. When we can dwell in the place where the mind is balanced by body awareness, we can harness its power. Our mind is meant to interpret and analyze but we allow it to run rampant and then we disconnect from our bodies. When we disconnect from our body and our mind becomes too difficult to control, we find ways to distract through food, alcohol, television, social media, drugs, shopping, smoking, worrying, planning. Overthinking is a way of disconnecting. Avoidance becomes a habit.

When we can midwife our own healing, and unearth our essential selves by allowing and accepting all of ourselves, we can emerge with the potential to create and lead and forge into what we are destined for. When we heal ourselves emotionally, we heal our fracture. This emotional-spiritual healing allows our bodies to heal in unseen ways that we can't begin to understand yet. Our own healing also facilitates the healing of others as we model, teach and inform. We also have the potential to heal across time, past and future generations. Transformation begins with us.

Hawthorn

Rich in folklore and tradition, and a member of the rose family, Hawthorn "gladdens" the heart while calming the nerves. Hawthorn is one of my favorite remedies for sadness, grief and loss or during times when the heart needs a bit of extra protection. It has a long history of use by cultures from around the globe for healing humanity's afflictions. Medicinally, the flowers, leaves and berries are all used and have properties that are beneficial to the circulatory system. It is wondrous in its capacity to bring balance and comfort to the heart and helps ease symptoms of nervous unrest and emotional or spiritual heartache. Hawthorn's berries make an excellent tinctures, jellies and decoctions. The flowers and leaves are used for tea infusions.

Crataegus spp., Hawthorn
"It's never too late to have a happy childhood."

Chapter 3:
THE GOOD GIRL

Before I am your daughter, your sister, your aunt, niece, or cousin, I am my own person, and I will not set fire to myself to keep you warm.

– ELIZABETH GRACELY

For many women, being a good girl is the single most common thing that holds us back and causes us pain in life. For many women, it can take a lifetime to break free of this mindset. Family and teachers have stressed being a good girl for decades, and it's the single most common thing that holds women back as we pursue our dreams. This desire to "be good" keeps us from pushing, from aspiring, and to challenge the system when we need to. This idea is still prevalent for young girls today. What does the result of this teaching look like in every-day life? Young women, girls, and grown women have the urge to please everyone, they feel as though they're never good enough, are hesitant to express their true feelings, and find it hard to say no. They feel exhausted by trying to meet the demands of everyone around us. Sound familiar?

Getting free of this mentality offers us a better chance to live not according to other people's expectations but according to our own guidance, and feel more worthy, whole, joyful, and fulfilled as a result.

Before we explore how to be free of the people-pleasing nice girls in us, we need to explore the societal norms of where it begins.

According to Reshma Saujani, author of *Girls Who Code*, there is a bravery deficit that is at the core of women's underrepresentation in government, law, STEM (science, technology, engineering, and math,) and the C-suite. Through her work in teaching girls to code, Saujani has observed the tendency for girls to be people pleasers, to not rock the boat, and to be perfect, and this socialization has had consequences in how women show up later in life. Saujani speaks about how important it is for us to teach girls what we teach boys: to be brave, to take risks, and that failure is okay. We must teach girls to be resilient and to try, even if they might fail. In other words, to be brave rather than perfect.

The subtle (and not-so-subtle) messages mainstream culture teaches girls that perfection, youth, and beauty are measurements of value, and that girls should be helpful, good, and nice. They are setting women up to hold themselves back for fear that they might be judged or criticized. It is a setup for women to dismiss their own needs and take care of everyone else around them before they take care of themselves. To say yes when they really don't want to for fear that they might disappoint someone. For not standing up for themselves to avoid hurting someone's feelings or ruffling feathers.

Think back to your days in elementary school and how you were praised. Were you praised for being "smart" or "good"? Boys are often praised for trying hard or being brave. Because of how girls are praised, they will often avoid challenges, try to look smart, stop raising their hands, and give up easily if they can't be perfect on the first try. Boys tend to persist even if they experience setbacks, believing that with continued effort, they will master an endeavor. As girls, we are socialized to aspire to perfection. We are rewarded and praised for being "good." As women, we are scared about not getting it right.

The good news: Women can increase their resilience factor by learning bravery, taking risks, and developing confidence in the face of challenges and failures. What I have seen in my work is that after years of trying to be "good," many women have lost touch with their true selves. Reconnecting with our true selves provides us with an internal compass that guides our truth. Of course, we will still encounter challenges, we will fail, and we will feel shame and vulnerability; however, when we accept ourselves at our deepest core level, we are able to build resilience, bravery, and a belief in our destiny. We learn from the setbacks and try again because nothing and no one is more important than who we know we must be.

We cannot surrender our own joy to feel more

dependable. To feel fully alive and purposeful, we must experience our own joy. Believing in yourself means sharing your most authentic self with the world. This requires you to be who you are. Don't look for evidence that you aren't good enough. You will find it because that is what you are focused on. Stop looking for confirmation that you aren't smart enough or don't fit in.

A client initially contacted me because, although she was a senior executive for a large corporation, managing large teams and making global decisions, she was miserable in her career. When we began working together, she was 52 years old. She had started with the company after completing her PhD in strategic management and had been there nearly 20 years. In our first session, she told me, "I feel like I'm living someone else's life." She was right. When she reflected on the ways she used to explore and play as a child, she remembered her connection to nature and how she used to spend hours down by the creek behind the house she grew up in, collecting stones and twigs and building fairy houses.

When she was 10, her family experienced a massive financial setback and lost everything, including the home with the creek where she used to explore. She felt her parents' stress. She had been taught to be responsible and well-behaved. She had been praised at home and at school for being tidy, sitting quietly, following instructions, and completing tasks. After her family's financial collapse, the messages got clearer about how her parents were expecting her to exhibit good behavior. As an adult looking back, she could see that her parents were feeling shame and needed her and her sister to present an external image that the family was still worthy of acceptance.

This pressure to carry the responsibility for the family's reputation drove her to achieve in school and succeed in her career, which she did beautifully…to the detriment of her true self. Eventually she reached a tipping point where it became intolerable to continue to deny the hunger for more.

Because we are fundamentally social creatures who form our identities in relation to our families, communities, and peers, we adapt ourselves for acceptance. Girls especially learn to be responsive to the needs of others, which is not a bad thing unless it sacrifices our universal selves.

Universal Self vs. Societal Self

Your universal self is the essence of who you are, your pure identity that existed before birth, before any environmental influences or social conditioning. This original self defines your unique quirks, longings, predilections, reactions and forms your uniqueness and individuality. Your universal self is not changed or affected by how you were parented, who you were raised by or where you grew up. To be rooted in your purpose, the first and critical first step is for you to get back in touch with your universal self. This is the part of you that must guide you towards your destiny and your joy.

Contrarily, your societal self has developed because

of social conditioning and the process of adapting to the expectations of family, teachers, and peers. This is the part of us that needs to be accepted and liked for our very survival. As babies, our survival depends on the adults that care for us and to ensure that care we modify ourselves for maximum acceptance. Human babies are born knowing that their very survival depends on the good will of the grown-ups around them. Because of this, we are literally designed to please others. The societal self is the part of you that craved being told she was a "good girl."

The formation of our societal selves also builds the skills we need to effectively function within cultural norms—we learn how to speak, keep personal hygiene, dress appropriately, read, raise our hands in class, dance, take our turn—the appropriate behaviors that will earn social approval. Our societal selves are critical to our ability to reach goals like completing a degree or landing a job. The problem is when the societal self dominates, and the universal self no longer has a voice.

As Martha Beck says in *Finding Your Own North Star*, "Your essential self was the part of you that smiled for the first time as a baby. Your social self is the part of you that noticed how much your mother loved that smile. Your essential self wants passionately to become a doctor; the social self struggles through organic chemistry and applies to medical school. Your essential self yearns for time in nature; your social self buys the right hiking shoes."

Typically, the societal self is the one in the driver's seat, and the universal self doesn't even make it into the car. The societal self has dominated for so long, making choices according to what is most socially acceptable, that the universal self can't even be heard. That is until a cataclysmic life event happens which causes the societal self to collapse.

The suppression of the universal self is why almost every woman I have worked with has ultimately sought help. Often for years, they have been feeling dissatisfaction with life which has not shifted despite the perseverance at being a better person, new yoga classes, a healthier diet, more volunteerism, and taking on more responsibility at work. Striving to be even more acceptable only makes things worse as it fuels the internal conflict between the universal self's need to pursue core longings and the societal self's requirement not to upset anyone. The dissatisfaction eventually turns to restlessness, anxiety, numbness, self-doubt, even despair.

If our life choices and behaviors are motivated by the desire to keep another person happy, we will lose the connection with our universal self. Without that connection, it's not possible to be deeply happy. Betraying yourself is selling your soul. So how do we calm down our societal self so that we can hear what our universal self is screaming for?

Tools and Exercises - 1

Daily Meditation

The practice of daily meditation carves out a time to quiet your mind, calm your societal self, and connect into the deep well of inner peace inside so that you can hear the whisperings of your universal self. With regular practice, you will find resistance releasing and a sense of clarity about who you really are and what you most desire. Letting go of the societal self and connecting with your universal self allows you to experience what psychologist Mihaly Csikszentmihalyi calls being in the "flow." Ultimately you will begin to experience this flow feeling whenever you are showing up in daily life as your universal self and connecting from that place with the people around you and the task in front of you.

Developing a regular meditation practice is very individual. You need to find the type of meditation that works best for you, the most conducive time of day and the location that best fits your needs. There are many different types of meditation and you'll ultimately find the one that most resonates for you. I'm certainly not a meditation instructor however I will describe the "mantra meditation" as the technique that I have found works for me. A mantra is a word or phrase that is silently repeated during meditation. I use *OM* throughout my inhale, *AH* at the apex of my breath, and *HUM* during my exhale. If have found this more effective than using

English language words as my mind doesn't attach any meaning with them so they don't trigger thoughts. The whole idea is to quiet the mind, so we can access our universal self.

Once you have a mantra selected, the next step is to find a quiet location where you won't be disturbed with comfortable place to sit. You can sit on the floor, or on a chair or sofa. It's important to sit upright with your spine straight. Being comfortable is the priority though. You can support yourself with a cushion, pillow or blanket if you like. Sitting is preferable to lying down to prevent falling asleep. I find it helpful to meditate in the same place every day and at the same time. I find the mornings my most powerful meditation time of day because I'm not as tired as I might be in the afternoon or evening. I am much calmer and more centered, resilient, peaceful and conscious during the day, when I meditate in the morning.

Now It's Time to Begin Meditating.

- Gently close your eyes and begin by taking a few unusually deep breaths, inhaling slowly through your nose an exhaling out your mouth. After several of these deeper breaths, continue to breathe normally, in and out through your nose.

- Begin repeating your mantra silently to yourself, softly, gently, and relaxed. You don't need to match your mantra with your breath although I have found it to be very helpful to do so. Silently repeat "OM" during your inhale. Pause momentarily at the end of your inhale and silently repeat "AH." Then silently repeat "HUM" on your exhalation. Allow your breath to find its own rhythm and the repetition of your mantra to become effortless. You can imagine that it's being whispered in your ear.

- When thoughts appear in your mind, once you have noticed them, simply turn your attention back to your mantra and following your breath.

- Continue this process for 20 to 30 minutes. Even a few minutes of daily meditation is beneficial, play with this and find the amount of time that works best for you. I like to set a gentle timer (you don't want to be startled out of meditation) so that my mind can relax and not turn to worrying thoughts about the time. After the timer goes off, spend a few minutes relaxed with your eyes closed before resuming activity.

- I allow for an additional 10 minutes after meditation to write in my journal. For the same reason that the shower is one of the best places for creative ideas to pop up, intuitive messages will come up during meditation and I find it helpful to jot these down before moving on with my day.

Boundaries and Conflicts

Women with a "good girl" tendency are often inclined to avoid conflict in relationships at work and at home. Conflict is natural part of a healthy relation-ship. Conflict gives us an opportunity to show up in our truth, speak up about how we feel and what we need. Yet many women, including myself, feel great discomfort when someone disagrees with us or is angry with us for any reason. To avoid this, we hint at difficult issues rather than being direct about them or we disguise difficult topics in conversation or procrastinate discuss-ing them. By not expressing our true feelings or stating our needs, we put ourselves on the back burner and by doing so, we can end up feeling dismissed, controlled, and suppressed.

In the next chapter I will describe how to shift our ingrained beliefs that create blind spots for us. With the women that I have coached, the most common limiting beliefs that come up around conflict include:

- Good relationships should be harmonious, and conflict is a sign that something is wrong. We should agree.

- When someone is upset with me, it's not safe.

- I need to rescue someone when they are upset and help them to feel better.

- I shouldn't say anything that might hurt someone else's feelings.

The reality is that difference of opinion is natural and usually there is no absolute truth. Often in a disagree-ment, there is truth in what both individuals feel and acknowledging the other person's experience and having them acknowledge ours is what is necessary. Every adult is fully capable of taking care of him or herself and even if they are feeling a difficult emotion, they don't need us to save them. It is entirely normal for each of us to feel strong emotions and they don't need to be avoided.

The next time you can feel the uncomfortable anticipation of a difficult conversation or potential conflict, ground down into your body, feel your feet on the ground, and keep breathing deeply. Give yourself loving compassion and support by telling yourself, "You're safe. You can do this. It's vitally important to express your truth." Your job is to stay in your body, breathing, speak from the vantage point of your own experience and when the other person speaks, deeply listen, try not to react, and reflect back what you have heard them say about how they are feeling, without making them wrong. You don't need to accept the responsibility for how they are feeling. Everyone is 100% responsible for their own reactions. Do take the responsibility for speaking up and saying what is true for you. Take responsibility of what you think, how you feel, and what you want.

I have a client who owned a business with her siblings that had been in the family for over forty years. She carried the burden of responsibility for her siblings' ownership in the business, a burden that had weighed heavily on her for twenty years. She sacrificed her own desires and needs for two decades, for the sake of her family. By the time we started working together, it had taken a toll on her physical and emotional wellbeing.

When we isolated her belief that she would let them down if she spoke up and stated what she wanted, to buy them out so she wouldn't be responsible for their inheritance, she became aware of her tendency to rescue other people at her own expense.

Although it was the scariest thing she had ever done, she set up a meeting with her siblings and told them her decision. This brave act of speaking her truth, not only healed herself, it healed generational family dysfunction. She found an authentic part of her universal self that brought a new sense of relief, peace, and strength.

Being in this kind of integrity with ourselves, even when it feels hard, is the essence of establishing proper boundaries. Over committing to please or rescue others means we sacrifice ourselves and this eventually wears us down. Many women believe "I have to do everything, or nothing will get done." Doing it all can lead to burnout, depression, and getting sick. This striving, whether it shows up as trying to be a supermom, overachieving at work, or volunteering on multiple committees, is how women tend to overcompensate for the insecurity they feel, seeking validation through external accomplishments. This was my strategy for decades until I got so depleted that I just couldn't do it anymore.

I have also observed how when women don't have clear boundaries and stand up for them, they often develop resentment for those around them. When our needs are perpetually denied, we can tend to feel angry with the very people who we are prioritizing over ourselves. Conversely, when we make ourselves and our needs a priority, we have the energy bandwidth and emotional capacity to be kinder and more compassionate. In *Daring Greatly*, Brené Brown says, "The most compassionate people that I've ever interviewed... happened to be the most boundaried. They happened to be the people who had very, very clear boundaries about what they were willing to do, what they were not willing to do, what they were willing to take on, and what they were not willing to take on... I think it is much easier to be compassionate when we feel respected, and almost impossible to feel compassionate, and feel empathic for people when we feel like we're being taken advantage of or when we're being sucked dry."

Saying "No, I can't do that," can feel incredibly uncomfortable as we begin to practice honoring our boundaries. Choosing to feel that discomfort in the moment is an act of self-integrity and self-care in the long term.

Learning the difference between what "yes" and "no" feels like to our universal selves is the foundation of establishing clear boundaries. Calming the societal self is the first step in discerning this difference. The practice of saying "no" when our universal self is feeling it, requires a healthy balance of our societal and universal selves. A balance that comes from not just hearing the voice but heeding it. It can feel scary at first but with practice, the voice gets clearer and we get stronger.

The voice of the universal self is our inner wisdom

and can only be heard / felt through the body. Because it is a subtle, sublime whisper, we must choose to hear it. The choice to calm the mind and the societal self, connect in our hearts and bodies and listen to the intuitive truth of what bubbles up, despite the waves of fear that might wash through us.

Be Your Most Powerful Self

I used to think it would motivate me if I noticed everything I was doing wrong so I constantly reminded myself of how I was falling short, how I could do better. That is what my well-meaning parents had done after all and who was I to imagine that there was a more self-affirming way to be my best? So, I adopted that technique and used it through my early adult years.

As children, our key survival mechanism is to be accepted. If we are accepted, there's a better chance of our survival. We won't be cast out to fend for ourselves. So, we integrate the messages we receive from parents, teachers and peers as the absolute truth and we modify our true nature accordingly in order to become more acceptable. As miraculously beautiful infants, we aren't thinking thoughts like "I'm not pretty enough" or "I'm not as smart as he is."

As we get older we hear how we should behave and we believe what we are told. These messages become a running tape in our minds that continues playing until we begin to question it. These were the thoughts and beliefs that kept me small and kept me being a good girl.

As a young woman, I subconsciously accepted social and cultural beliefs about how I should behave, which kept me even smaller. Even though I have always seen myself as a rebel and a change-maker, I still held in my societal self the expectation that I should behave in specific culturally acceptable ways. I trusted that if I came on too strong I might not be as likeable or appealing and might be perceived as a "bitch." Again, the primal need to survive.

I often didn't celebrate my successes because no matter how well I did, I believed I could and should do better. This was what I told myself. I can remember squelching feelings of pride when I reached goals so that I wouldn't become egotistical or over-confident. People might not like me if I didn't stay humble and powerless.

Not allowing myself to believe in how powerful I truly am, kept me drained, flat, unhappy, and well, small. It was safer or, so I thought. Being accepted was more important than feeling good about myself. That strategy worked until it didn't work. I got fed up with not feeling good enough.

When we spend our energy telling ourselves we're not doing good enough, we have very little time and energy left to do what we were meant to do. We end up working even harder to do better and have less and less time and energy. We read more self-help books. We work longer hours and take less time off. We watch what other people are doing and invariably find someone who is doing better than we are. This makes us feel awful and in the pursuit of feeling better about ourselves, we buckle down and try even harder. We look everywhere for validation of who we are except the one place we need to look: inside.

Are you playing small? Tendencies of small players:

- Deny compliments and don't allow yourself to believe them

- Keep in check any feelings of success or only notice what you did wrong, so you don't feel too good about yourself

- Have fears about not being accepted if you shine your brightest because you might scare people away

- Shrinking yourself energetically so that other people won't feel insecure around you; putting yourself down when talking to other people

- Internalize the voices of parents and teachers

- Feel you don't deserve the things you want or dream about

- Stay in relationships and jobs that aren't working and are so depleting that it feels like you are dying a slow death

- Feel like a victim in your own story

- Give your power away, because you fear conflict

- Procrastinate and avoid the very things that will get you closer to your dreams

- Seek approval and validation from others

- Tend to be a perfectionist
- Have a wounded belief system that accepts "I am not [fill in the blank] enough."
- Feel separate or isolated
- Compare yourself to others to see how you fall short or appear better
- Feel like you never fit in

We live (in western cultures) according to a belief system that if we are to find happiness or success, it is contingent on having more of something—better opportunities, a higher-paying job, more wealth and beauty, to be thinner, younger or older. Reach, stretch, and push. Always seek more. This infers that, who we are, what we have, is not enough. I'm not saying that we shouldn't have dreams and goals that we are working towards. What I'm talking about is the fundamental belief that we aren't good enough already.

"If I lose these 20 pounds, then I'll be attractive enough."

"Once I get that degree, I'll be credible enough."

"When I have a baby, I'll finally be happy."

"If I get that promotion, I'll be making more money and then I'll be able to enjoy life."

> *Argue for your limitations and, sure enough, they're yours.*
>
> — RICHARD BACH

So how can we be our biggest, most powerful and radiant selves, yet also remain compassionate and vulnerable?

In accepting our thoughts as the gospel truth, we are allowing them to limit us. We are putting our thoughts in control of who we are and yet these very same insidious thoughts were always meant to keep us in line. So, we smother our light with negativity, in the form of fear and doubt. We each have so much more potential than we allow ourselves to believe.

> *Our deepest fear is not that we are inadequate.*
> *Our deepest fear is that we are powerful beyond*
> *measure. It is our light, not our darkness that*
> *most frightens us. We ask ourselves, who am*
> *I to be brilliant, gorgeous, talented, fabulous?*
> *Actually, who are you not to be?*
>
> — MARIANNE WILLIAMSON

I have worked hard on all the ways I used to keep myself small. I now know and appreciate that I am unique, that there is only one me. I have stopped comparing myself with others (well most of the time) because when I do, I am dimming my own light. To do my part, to offer the world my gifts and talents, I need to shine as brightly as I can. I have learned that the only person I need to listen to is me. I accept that I feel the way I do instead of believing I should feel some other way. Every single minute of every single day, my work is about noticing what thoughts I choose to believe. I am the author of my own story. This is the only way that I can be the best me, the biggest and most beautiful and radiant me, right now. And the only one I need to please and be accepted by is me. My opinion is the only one that matters.

Every single one of us is unique and special and the world needs each of us to live up to our full potential. Even when it feels scary, we need to just feel the fear and do it anyway. Discovering our unique gifts, what we are born to offer the world and what we feel passionate about is what we are here to do. I'm not better or worse than anyone else. I am not separate from anyone or anything. We all have within us a divine light, a little piece of God. Each of us is special and beautiful and enough. This is the radical self-acceptance and enoughness that is the theme of my story now.

By allowing my light to shine it's brightest, I am doing my own healing work. I need to heal myself before I can do my part to heal the planet.

Playing small doesn't serve the world. When we shine, we unconsciously give other people the permission to shine too. When we are liberated from our own fear, our presence liberates others. Suffering is the doorway to our liberation. We begin this liberation by looking at and questioning each thought. Thought by thought as we release our belief in them, we get lighter and lighter.

There is no passion to be found playing small - in settling for a life that is less than the one you are capable of living.

— NELSON MANDELA

Tools and Exercises - 2

Discerning "YES" from "NO"

Because the body is the loud speaker for our soul, I am going to walk you through how to "hear" your body speaking the voice of your universal self. You'll want your journal handy for this. This is a quick overview of how to create a "compass" from your body's reactions to both negative and positive experiences or even tasks on your To Do List so that you can discern "yes" from "no." Learning this tool will allow you to use your body as the guide to what your universal self needs and wants instead of relying on your mind or your societal self, i.e. someone else's expectations. Our inner wisdom speaks to us through our bodies, not with words but through felt sensations and images.

Begin by preparing yourself for meditation, as outlined earlier. Gently close your eyes and begin by taking a few unusually deep breaths, inhaling slowly through your nose and exhaling out your mouth. After several of these deeper breaths, continue to breathe normally, in and out through your nose. Turn your awareness to your body. Make a mental connection with each part of your body, starting by feeling your feet touching the floor and your seat being supported by the chair beneath it. Move your awareness up your legs, your seat in the chair, up through your torso, up the back of your neck, across the top of your head, your face, across your shoulders, down your arms and your fingers. As you move slowly through your body, breath into each part, noting any tension and feeling it relax.

Now, think about a negative experience you had at some point in your life. Specifically, think of something you would never ever want to go through again, a truly painful time that brought you a great deal of suffering. Scan your entire body noting any physical sensation as you remember this time. Make a mental note describing these sensations in as much detail as possible. Notice the sensation, note where you feel it in your body and describe it with qualities like heavy or light, warm, cold, spiky, or smooth, big, small, tight, constricted. Notice what shape it is. Is it a ball, blob, or does it have sharp edges? Does it have a color? Give the sensation a name. Give the sensation a rating on a scale from -10 to zero. How awful did it feel, as bad as -10 or was it more like -8, with zero being completely neutral? Shake that off (literally shake your arms and legs—this is how horses release stress) and take a few deep breaths.

The next step is to think of one of the most beautiful and happy moments in your life. A time when you felt euphoric and exhilarated. This might be a time that you were falling in love or when you climbed to the top of a mountain, or rode a horse on the beach, or when your child was born. Once you have the memory in mind, take yourself back there and remember it with all your senses. Recall the quality of the light, the feeling of the air on your skin, the warmth of the person you are with, the smell of trees or flowers, the sound of the wind or the ocean. What is the sensation you feel in your body now? Where do you feel it? Mentally describe the sensation in as much detail as possible. This might feel something like light or expansive. Or peaceful. Give this positive sensation a name. Rate this sensation on a scale from zero to +10, with zero being neutral and +10 being the peak of bliss.

When you feel complete with this, take a few deep breaths, wiggle your toes and fingers and when you're ready, open your eyes. Take a few minutes to write down what you experienced.

These sensations are likely the way your body communicates "No" and "Yes" to you. Now you just need to start paying attention to them. We have neural nets in other parts of our bodies besides our brain. There are neural nets in our abdomen ("gut level feelings"), and around our heart ("love" or "broken heart"). Our bodies tell us all the time whether we truly mean "Yes" or "No." When you feel a clear "No," ask yourself "What do I need right now?" Like anything, practice hones ability. The more you honor your universal self by speaking your truth and stating what you want and need, you will not only develop your own empowerment, it will empower those around you and create relationships built on integrity.

Remember that fulfilling other people's projections of who we are, rather than living in our own truth leads to the undervaluing of ourselves, making it difficult to feel confident. Empowerment is available to those who live their truth.

Nettle

Herb students have often asked me, "If you had to pick one herb, what would it be?" Without a doubt, Stinging Nettle. Nettle is one of my five most favorite medicinals. It is a powerhouse of healing and highly nutritive, rich in vitamins A and C, and minerals, particularly calcium and iron. Along with a plethora of health benefits from boosting immunity, easing allergies, aiding the liver, strengthening the muscular-skeletal system, and easing joint pain, Nettle is great for when you feel worn-out and drained by doing too much for others. It also provides energetic protection, giving you time to recharge and reset your body and mind. Nettle, dried or fresh, makes a delicious tea.

Urtica dioica, Stinging Nettle

When neurosurgeon Eben Alexander went into a coma caused by a bacterial infection in his brain and had a profound near-death experience, he received three messages in the spirit world that he describes in his book *Proof of Heaven*:

1. You are loved and cherished, dearly and forever.
2. You have nothing to fear.
3. There is nothing you can do wrong.

There is no right way or wrong way, only YOUR way.

Chapter 4:
NEW BELIEFS

The truth you believe and cling to makes you unavailable to hear anything new.

— Pema Chodron

Your thoughts create your reality. I was first introduced to this concept in 1992 by Wayne Dyer and it has been the central theme of my self-work as well as my coaching work since then. The Law of Attraction says that when we are feeling a negative emotion, we are resisting something that we want, and that creating positive thoughts will make our vibrational frequency higher which will attract good things to us. Therefore, we must intentionally develop thoughts that will attract what we want. Yet how do we do this if we are resisting something we want? Why would we resist something we want?

If your mind is choosing not to have what you truly want it is because it is believing that a limiting factor is a problem.

When I work with women entrepreneurs, the most common thing I hear them say is "I'm just not smart enough to do this." Each time I hear this, I find it ironic because frequently these are women who not only have graduate degrees but have launched successful businesses. How and why does this happen?

Herein lies what I believe is one of the key reasons why women hold themselves back.

Thought Work

Earlier, I discussed The Fracture and the development of the Societal Self. The messages we receive as children, from well-meaning adults, can become the voice of our inner critic as adults. We believe these judgements to be the gospel truth because we took them on without question and integrated them as we wove the fabric of our self-identity. The voice of our inner critic, telling us what we should do, feel, and say, is associated with survival instincts that we no longer need. This voice blocks us from hearing, trusting and heeding our intuition. We aren't able to perceive the messages of our inner wisdom or we do and choose to ignore them.

Let's examine the process of how our thoughts drive our behavior.

A **Circumstance** or facts drive our **Thoughts** about it which drives our **Feelings,** which drive our **Behavior** or action. We can't change the circumstance, but we can change our feelings and reactions to it, as well as our behavior. We do this by reframing our thoughts.

Circumstance: These are the facts about a situation over which we have little or no control. For example: *My* *husband left me. My son dropped out of college. My business is losing money. I lost my job.*

Thoughts: This is how we interpret the circumstance through our own lens, and what we make it mean. *I can't go on without my marriage. My son is a loser. I'm going to lose everything and be destitute. No one will hire me.*

Feelings: The emotional reactions to the thoughts—the anger, sadness, fear, disappointment, anxiety, annoyance, hopelessness, frustration, resentment, etc. Uncomfortable feelings are clear indicators that we are believing something that may not be true for us.

Behavior: This is the action that is driven by the feelings. We choose to respond to our feelings in multiple ways. In many cases, we might try to avoid the feeling if it is particularly uncomfortable. For example, sleeping all day, binge eating, screaming at someone, hiding at home, alcohol, drugs, and other addictions (social media, television, etc.)

Self-limiting thoughts also follow this same pattern as we relive circumstances from the past. We all have experienced pain in our lives, something that happened in childhood, last month, or even yesterday. How often we play them out, over and over in our minds, causing ourselves the same pain each time. The past is over but unfortunately, in our minds we recreate it each time, with the same thought, the same reaction and often the same choice because of how we have made ourselves feel. The story told over in our mind creates an emotional response with feelings such as sadness, anger, insecurity, or guilt, as well as physical sensations such as tightness in the chest or discomfort in the pit of our stomach. These feelings also instruct us to behave in a certain way. Learning how to create a space between feelings and behavior helps us gain new perspective, allowing us to see our problems as separate from ourselves so new choices can be made.

I've seen this pattern with clients who turn to food or exercise or alcohol or social media for comfort. We may tell ourselves a story about this circumstance, reliving it over and over each time we think about it, believing each painful thought we have.

The integral piece in this progression is that the lens through which we interpret a circumstance is predetermined by the beliefs that we have established as truth, through the course of our life. The way we navigate through our lives largely depends on these beliefs. They determine our thoughts and how we feel and make decisions, and every part of our life over which we have control. Freedom comes from transforming the way we view the past and rewriting these old mental stories. This is how we shift how we feel, how we react, our behavior, actions, and the choices we make. Our thoughts truly do create our reality, for better, or for worse. Changing our thinking is one of the most powerful tools we have, to change our lives. Our work is to dissolve the thoughts and feelings that make us miserable.

Tools and Exercises

Overwriting Negative Beliefs

In *Loving What Is,* Byron Katie teaches us how to question the thoughts that are causing us suffering and driving our reactions. Katie calls it "The Work," a process of inquiry that questions beliefs about ourselves, other people and about life. This simple process traces unhappiness back to the thought or belief that triggered it, questions that belief and then opts for a more supportive belief. The Work teaches us to identify and question the thoughts causing our suffering and consists of four questions and the turnarounds that clarify a more supportive viewpoint.

I have used this technique with many clients over the years and have observed that not only does The Work reduce stress, anger, anxiety and fear, it creates more inner peace and clarity which opens new levels of emotional and mental bandwidth, giving them the confidence to move forward on projects.

Since the 1960's, psychologists have been saying that automatic negative thoughts sabotage us and create a vicious cycle of suffering mindsets. We get stuck in these old neural pathways. Like well-travelled roads, our brains tend towards these negative thoughts, again and again.

Before I began doing this work, I assumed when a negative thought popped into my head it was an accurate reflection of the way things were. However, by questioning these thoughts, I created another point of view and a new vantage point for my brain. There's always another point of view available if we are ready to have an open mind.

Increasing evidence of the brain's plasticity suggests we can disrupt this destructive cycle and activate new neural pathways that are healthier, more self-supportive, positive and productive. Our brains don't stop developing in childhood and as adults we can learn to stop our mind from travelling down the well-trodden neural pathways by creating entirely new ones.

Step 1. Identify a self-limiting belief. The first step is becoming aware of our automatic negative thoughts. Byron Katie suggests that we begin by noticing how we are judging ourselves and others. For women who over-extend themselves, and end up feeling undervalued or unappreciated, disappointment and resentment can set in. Judgement of another may sound something like "He expects me to do everything!" Self-judgement is what stops women short from putting themselves and their work out in the world. I have observed the following as the most common self-limiting beliefs for women:

- Am I doing this right? (I'm not doing this right)
- Is this working? (This isn't working)
- Will I fail? (I am failing)
- Where is this going? (This isn't going anywhere)
- Am I ready to do this? (I'm not ready to do this, i.e. not enough training)

- Is this going to help anyone? (Nobody will want this)

- Do I have enough energy to do this? (I'm too old to be trying to do this)

- Have I done enough preparation for this? (I'm not smart enough)

- Is this going to make a difference? (It will never be good enough)

- Who will want this? (No one wants what I have to offer; people will think I'm stupid)

- Will I ever be able to finish this? (I'll never finish this)

- Why didn't I get this done last year? (I don't work hard enough)

- What's the point of doing this? (It will never be successful; I always fail; Nothing ever works for me)

Step 2. Create doubt around the negative belief. Once you have isolated your negative thought, the next step is to question it and create doubt around it. Katie created four questions for this:

1. Is it true? (Yes or no. If no, move to 3.)

2. Can you absolutely know that it's true? (Yes or no.)

3 How do you react, what happens, when you believe that thought?

4 Who would you be without the thought?

It's important to spend time on the third and fourth questions. Sit with the questions. Write about them.

For Question 3: When you believe the negative thought, how does it make you feel emotionally? How does it make you feel physically? What choices do you end up making because you feel that way? How do you treat yourself and other people?

For Question 4: If it was impossible for you to believe that thought, how would you feel, emotionally and physically? What choices would you make? How would you treat yourself and others?

Step 3. Overwrite the negative belief. There are several options for how to activate more self-supporting neural pathways. Katie suggests creating three different turnarounds for the original thought—turnaround to the self, to the other and to the opposite. Then finding at least three specific examples of how the turnaround is as true or truer than the original thought.

Coming up with as many specific examples of how the opposite turnaround is true is incredibly effective. If you can come up with 20 great, but shoot for at least 5 examples. Let's use "I'm not smart enough" as an example. The turnaround to the opposite is "I am smart enough." How many examples from your life, can you come up with to show that "I am smart enough" is as true or even truer than the original belief?

- I am smart enough to read this book
- I am smart enough to drive
- I am smart enough to get a job
- I am smart enough to balance my checkbook

- I am smart enough to get on the internet
- I am smart enough to read a map
- I am smart enough to use my smartphone

Your examples don't have to be elaborate for this to work. You don't have to think of the perfect examples for this to be powerful. Even the simplest ones will get your brain creating a new viewpoint. The important thing is that the examples are specific to you.

This process is what diverts the brain from the well-travelled negative neural pathway and begins building the new one. I explain to clients that the old pathway is like a super highway that our brain automatically goes down because it is habitual. You might have noticed how you automatically turn a certain direction when you are driving somewhere because that is the way you go to work every day, when you intended on turning in the opposite direction. Our brains work the same way.

Disbelieve poisonous thoughts that cause pain and distress. Vow to not believe any thought that causes suffering. Choose ease, joy, and freedom. Find evidence to refute thoughts like "I'm bad," or "I'm ugly," or "Nobody likes me."

As we begin creating a new neural pathway, it starts as a footpath. The more we use it, the more developed it becomes and eventually it turns into a highway while the old one gets cracked and overgrown with weeds. You might think that this takes a long time however to the contrary, I have seen immediate results when clients do this work. It's quite miraculous. As we turn the mind towards disproving a negative thought, we begin to feel freer and freer, until one day we can't imagine how we ever believed the original thought.

Be aware that it is quite tiring for your brain to do this work so allow yourself the time and space it deserves. I have found 45 minutes to be a good amount of time for all 3 steps, and an additional 15 minutes for your brain to adjust.

Lemon Balm

Because thought work can be taxing for the brain and perplexing for the psyche, I offer you Lemon Balm, *Melissa officinalis,* to assuage strain and lighten your spirit. It has a restorative and calming effect on the nervous system and I have found it very uplifting for clients who are experiencing melancholy.

Melissa has been recommended through the ages "to make the heart merry." In the 15th century, physician and alchemist Paracelsus claimed that *Melissa* could revitalize the body and called it the "elixir of life."

This lemony herb is a member of the mint family and is delightful as a tea. Lemon Balm is a wonderful remedy for colds, coughs, flu. It also helps soothe upset stomachs and eases nausea. It will help induce relaxation and improve sleep.

Lemon Balm is ideally suited during times of mental

distress and when we need to preserve mental clarity. It adds light to one's being.

Melissa officinalis, Lemon Balm

To pursue your life's calling, you must unlearn the thoughts that are blinding you to seeing what is already inside of you.

Chapter 5:
ORIGINAL MEDICINE

I think midlife is when the universe gently places her hands upon your shoulders, pulls you close, and whispers in your ear: I'm not screwing around. It's time. All of this pretending and performing — these coping mechanisms that you've developed to protect yourself from feeling inadequate and getting hurt — has to go.

Your armor is preventing you from growing into your gifts. I understand that you needed these protections when you were small. I understand that you believed your armor could help you secure all the things you needed to feel worthy of love and belonging, but you're still searching and you're more lost than ever.

Time is growing short. There are unexplored adventures ahead of you. You can't live the rest of your life worried about what other people think. You were born worthy of love and belonging. Courage and daring are coursing through you. You were made to live and love with your whole heart. It's time to show up and be seen.

—BRENÉ BROWN

Traditional cultures around the world have recognized that within each of us exists a unique array of qualities, gifts, talents, passions and longings that form our true identity and make us who we are. That each soul enters the world with a distinct, valuable and meaningful way to serve in the world. The most important thing we need to learn in life is who we are at our core and how we are intended to serve. Each of us must bring our unique vision to the world and find the courage to follow it through, wherever it may lead, through the dark forests, over the mountain crags, and across the vast desert. No one person is more special than any other because each of us possesses a unique expression that is essential. This is your hero's journey.

Your Original Medicine

We are most happy, most satisfied and fulfilled when we are offering our gifts to the world. When we are connected to our Original Medicine and approaching any moment in life from that place, we are at ease with ourselves and feel buoyant, even radiant. You were born with your Original Medicine, it has been with you, always.

An inevitable part of growing up as the societal self develops in response to pressures from the people around us, is that we lose touch with our Original Medicine. We work so hard to fit in and belong that our work later in life becomes a process of excavating and unearthing our originality so that we can express our unique gifts.

For me, this process of rediscovery is fundamental to personal empowerment and overcoming self-doubt. Understanding and acknowledging how we are distinctively unique is fundamental to personal power, strength and confidence.

To reestablish a connection with your Original Medicine, think back to your childhood, to times when you felt free. When you ran, played hide-and-seek, skipped rope, climbed trees and built forts. As children, we naturally gravitate towards the activities that we excel at. What did you do as a child that made you feel good, powerful, and free? What activity made time stand still for you, when you lost track of time?

Peak moments in life also reveal a connection with our Original Medicine. A peak experience is a moment accompanied by a euphoric mental state. This concept was originally developed by Abraham Maslow in 1964, who describes peak experiences as "rare, exciting, oceanic, deeply moving, exhilarating, elevating experiences that generate an advanced form of perceiving reality and are even mystic and magical in their effect upon the experimenter." These peak moments create the experience of reaching one's full potential which generates an ecstatic, blissful feeling.

Think of times in your life when you were at your absolute best and felt a deep sense of joy, expansiveness, and freedom. Was there a time, maybe for even a brief moment, where everything just felt right, and you felt like you had found your place in the world? How were you expressing your deepest self in that moment? This is a clue that you were connected to your Original Medicine during that experience.

Imagination

Everything that exists in life was imagined first. The power to imagine is the greatest human capacity and our lives are created through our imagination. We imagine ourselves into being, whether we are aware of it, or not. Our Original Medicine, the unique blueprint of our soul allows us the ability to imagine life in ways unique to everyone else.

Our dreams, those things we know intuitively, and visions are the inspiration for what wants to happen. Returning to imaginative ways of being is the truest path to yourself, your calling and a meaningful life. We sense our longings, resolve our issues, and visualize new possibilities, all within our imagination. We then create what we have already imagined.

When I was getting reacquainted with my Original Medicine, I remembered how huge my night dreams had always been for me. I recalled that I have always received powerful guidance through my dreams since I was little, and I still do, although during the years I was armored up and protecting myself, I rarely had a dream that I remembered. When I began the work of reconnecting with my body, meditating, and understanding (and accepting) my uniqueness, my dreams became clear and potent messengers of divine guidance.

No one else can tell us where we should go or what we should do because they don't possess our personal magic. Your real guidance may speak to you in different ways—trying to send you messages—through dreams, through clues, through coincidences, through déjà vu, through intuition, through destiny, through surprising waves of attraction and reaction, through the chills that run up your arms and the hair that stands up on the back of your neck, through the excitement of something new and exciting, or through ideas that keep you awake all night. When we learn to believe in ourselves, we begin to trust in this guidance.

Children demonstrate the inner qualities of their soul and may suddenly display a talent or wisdom beyond their age. Children dwell in their true nature and through play will demonstrate their unique gifts. Childhood play is free, joyful, and timeless. These feelings of expansiveness and freedom through play are like a compass leading us to our Original Medicine.

Tools and Exercises

Life Experiences Made You Who You Are

Each of us is shaped by our life experiences. Good and bad, everything that we have gone through has altered us and shaped us into who we are today. Our thoughts, attitude, aspirations, and expectations are all shaped by our experiences. With each new experience, particularly the challenging ones, we gain a deeper understanding of ourselves.

Although I stress to clients to be in the now, and not to dwell on the past by talking about and rehashing painful memories over and over, for this exercise, I want you to take a journey through your past, exploring the most difficult circumstances and intense struggles of your life experience and what you learned about yourself because of them. We can begin to see our life's challenges as a gift when we can understand how they pointed us to a deeper sense of our strengths and resources and shifted us toward a new direction. We don't need to be victims of our life experiences when we view them for how they created new and positive circumstances and taught us about ourselves. The trials and tribulations we encounter are only learning opportunities and lessons that enable us to better handle future situations.

In your journal, down the left side of the page, make a list of specific memories from your childhood that felt painful. Leave plenty of room on the right side of the page for notes. A painful memory might conjure the experience of vulnerability, shame, being heartbroken, angry, sad, lonely, pessimistic, guilty, anxious, or jealous. I've heard a lot of pain around: the death of a family member, an ill or alcoholic parent, switching to a new school, bullying, coping with poverty, and varying types of abuse, neglect, and shaming.

Next to each of the memories, make notes about:

- How the pain helped to shape you into a better person, how it shaped your character and left you better and stronger

- How the experience directed you towards certain life choices

- How it helped you create a closer connection with others, humility, compassion or empathy

- How going through that challenge made you aware of a quality or strength that you have and how you have used that strength since

- Name and identify the quality inside of you that pulled you through those darkest times, that gave you the strength to persevere

Take a few minutes or hours for self-care when you've completed this exercise. Make yourself a cup of tea and curl up in front of the fire or go for a walk outside, breathing in the fresh air and feeling grateful for the trees that made it.

Mapping Your Peak Moments

We will continue our journaling as we take a different trip down memory lane. We are going to explore the peak experiences in your life that have also shaped who you are today. In these memories, you experienced moments of joy, being in the flow, and epiphany realizations. You may have experienced the sublime feeling of connection to yourself, other people, an animal, the place, or the surrounding nature, that made those experiences memorable and connected you with a capacity inside of you that made a difference somehow. It was a feeling that gave you a sense you were clicked in to something bigger than yourself.

Let's begin with a simple relaxation response. To be able to relive the positive sensations of our past, we need to begin by quieting the mind. Sit comfortably with your back straight. Put one hand on your chest and the other on your stomach. The key to deep breathing is to breathe deeply from the abdomen, getting as much fresh air as possible in your lungs. Breathe in through your nose. The hand on your stomach should rise. The hand on your chest should move very little. Exhale through your mouth, pushing out as much air as you can while contracting your abdominal muscles. Continue to breathe in through your nose and out through your mouth. Try to inhale enough so that your lower abdomen rises and falls. Count slowly as you exhale. As your body relaxes, so will your mind.

You will explore the "flow" moments in your life. Flow is the state of being in which time stands still, when you're totally engaged in an activity and you feel euphoric, or in the zone. That special state is when we lose track of time, when we fall into a gorgeous forgetting of ourselves and become completely merged with what we're doing. The activity may be running or gardening or writing or counseling or crunching numbers. Flow feels like:

- Experiencing complete involvement in an activity
- Feeling a sense of ecstasy or euphoria
- Having great inner clarity, knowing just what to do and how to do it
- Being totally calm and at peace
- Feeling as if time were standing still or disappearing in an instant

Make a list of the times of your life when you felt "in the flow." This can be even a moment, a tiny thing, but it felt like a +10 to your body and you experienced a sense of euphoria and inner clarity, total calm and peace, and a feeling as if time were standing still:

- Career highlights
- An awesome moment doing a sport or hobby
- A moment in a relationship with someone else where you felt really seen
- A moment with family that felt good
- A place you visited or travelled to that resonated deeply for you
- Your first memory at age 5, 6 or 7 that felt amazing and free
- A time in your teens
- A time in your 20's

For each memory ask yourself the following questions and write down what comes up:

- Why was that experience so good?

- What did it mean to me?
- What did it show about me and why was that significant?

When you've finished reflecting and writing about your peak moments, notice if there is a common theme between them. Is there a strength or quality you brought that is common to all of them? Can you notice a larger story about who you are? This theme or story may very well have nothing to do with what you do but may illustrate what your universal self deeply values and the part of you that must be honored and present in how you show up in your work and in your life. This quality of who you are when you are in the flow is the essence of your Original Medicine. How does your current life—career, relationships, and service—allow you to express this quality?

Universal Consciousness

New concepts have emerged in the field of neuroscience that suggest that consciousness is an inherent property of literally everything. In 2013, one of the leading experts on consciousness, neuroscientist Christof Koch, went to India to discuss his theories with the Dalai Lama. According to Koch, "The heart of consciousness is that it *feels* like something." After a full day of debate and discussion, His Holiness and Koch agreed: That consciousness is everywhere.

The idea of universal consciousness permeates ancient Greek philosophy, Buddhism, and paganism.

Consciousness is now an established branch of neuro-science. Together with Giulio Tononi, the originator of Integrated Information Theory, or ITT, created the modern theory of consciousness. Their work states that consciousness appears in all physical systems and that animals, plants, cells, bacteria, even protons are all conscious beings. Buddhism also considers land, sun, moon and stars as sentient beings.

By resting the mind, according to Buddhism, a medi-tator can develop an understanding and connection to everything else.

I offer this now as the prequel to my own Original Medicine story.

After the years of tailspin following my father's pass-ing, when I finally surfaced, I felt a disconnection from self and spirit. I became blatantly aware that some of the choices I had made were not aligned with my soul's purpose or my life calling, and that separateness was causing me suffering. Thus, began my own journey of self-discovery that led me to a reconnection with my Original Medicine.

As I mapped the flow moments of my life—from sensing the dolphins on the beach asking for help when I was 15 and later having this same connection with humpback whales in the Caribbean (fortunately they hadn't beached themselves,) to communicating with my Dad in dreams after his passing, dreaming about my unborn daughter, teaching the art and science of plant medicine, sensing the presence of my Mom after her death, visualizing locations for retreats as I was seeking them, connecting with animal and plant spirits, and a multitude of magical "knowings" experienced in meditations—my Original Medicine became crystal clear. I realized that I have an innate ability to feel the heart of universal consciousness that Koch wrote about and that this allows me to be a conduit of information and healing for others.

Through mapping my peak moments, I could pick up the thread of my unique gifts and through that process redefine myself from someone who felt unworthy of belonging into an intuitive and inspiring guide and mentor. I absolutely KNOW that you can do this as well and that you will have the experience of imagining yourself into being. The you that has always been there, and still is.

We all have the potential for a spiritually satisfying life with work that is exciting, engaging and heart-centered. Relationships that are intimate and vulnerable. A life where we experience beauty within and without and in which we feel feminine, strong, and free. Where we feel a deep connection to ourselves, to each other and to something bigger. Because of that potential to make a difference.

The potential for tapping into universal consciousness as well as seeing and dreaming into form happens when we shed the armor, question our limiting beliefs, reconnect with our bodies, and follow our true selves.

Original Medicine in Action

You know how some moments in life, no matter how long ago they were can be conjured up in our memories, in full color, as clearly as they just happened yesterday? What makes one experience more memorable than another?

For several years, I co-taught a training program for herbalists. As clearly as if it happened just this morning, I remember a specific moment from 1998, standing in front of a group of 20+women describing the connection between our respiratory system and the plant world. I was explaining the profound relationship between photosynthesis in plants and the physiology of our cellular respiration. In my description, I was marveling at the plethora of plant medicines that boost lung health and repair respiratory tissue. For a split second, time stopped. I can still see their eager faces, eyes filled with wonder and anticipation, spirits unfurling like the petals of a flower. A moment of awakening as an ancient memory was activated and they touched into a deep but forgotten connection to healing and plants. A knowing that resided beyond time and space, beyond physical dimension, in their genetic memories dating back to say 60,000 years ago, began to awaken in them. I recognize that moment as me being in sync with my Original Medicine. I was using my unique ability to connect with universal consciousness and stimulate a waking up for those women.

Using our gifts brings us closer to the divine. Conjuring that memory instantly brings a feeling of expansion and peace inside of me. No one person's medicine is better than another's. No work is more valuable than another's—do not diminish your role because you think bigger is better. The world needs all of us to bring forth our gifts. One kind heart has so much power to change the world. People in the community recognize in you a certain quality that only you have, and they come to you for that quality.

- Being a great mediator
- Ability to listen to others as they unload life's challenges
- Capacity to make people laugh
- Wisdom to see clearly

These are just a few examples of the God-like qualities that are innate within each of us. Every one of us is born with something that our community seeks us out for. Within you, your spirit has a quality that you are ordained to share with others. How do you find that quality?

- Heal the fractures and wounds of childhood, integrate their blessings, and peel away the armor that you created to protect yourself

- Get over being a good girl and doing anything because you think you should or have to do it

- Discern what your soul's loudspeaker (your body) is trying to tell you

- Dissolve the limiting beliefs that are stopping you from being in your power

- Get through the illusion that the only value by which to see yourself is through what you do, instead of who you are

- Recognize the spiritual energy that is thriving in you and realize that you are someone who has clear sight, or you're someone who's optimism endlessly flows, or you're someone who people come to because you make them feel good

- Follow the thread of your sacred power

- Accept the beautiful qualities in yourself

- Use the inspiration you feel when you are shining your light to guide life choices

Through this exercise, a client completely transformed her business and how it serves her clients. Through tracking her peak moments, she recalled a time during college when she had worked at a coffee house—one of the happiest times in her life. She remembered how she was able to connect from her heart with customers and draw them to their own hearts. Remembering this felt experience became a reminder of how she wanted to show up in every moment of her life.

When she understood the magnitude of her Original Medicine, that she has a special ability to "hold space" for other people that allows them to access their heart, it completely altered the way she managed her staff.

Before doing this work, she had been creating daily goals
for each of her employees and going over their perfor-
mance in weekly meetings—how well they did or more
commonly how they fell short. This was how she was
taught to manage for maximum productivity. Because
she also believed that she had to do everything perfectly,
every time one of her employees made even the smallest
error, she believed she was going to lose the business
and everything she had put into it. She was experiencing
high turnover of employees and an overall company
culture of resistance, bitterness, and discontent, which
was affecting her customers and ultimately her business.

She was at her wits end, in frustration and desper-
ation, because she had devoted her life to the business,
as well as most of her family's assets and was sensing
she was going to need to close the business. I really felt
her pain. After she connected with and allowed her
Original Medicine to be the focal point from which she
managed her team, she began to create an environment
where her employees felt seen in a way they never had
before. Instead of being the boss she thought she should
be, holding her employees accountable for their sales
goals, she was able to allow them to blossom and be their
best selves. And not only were they happier, they loved
working for her because they were able to express themselves and take authentic ownership in their roles. Team
members began innovating new ways for the company to
make a difference in the lives of their customers and their
community. Operating from her true self and modeling

that way of being, facilitated the potential for her staff to do the same. This is how one leader can change a company culture and change the world.

Tools and Exercises

Dream Journal

One of the most potent practices for cultivating self-awareness is dream journaling. I consistently marvel at the synchronicities that magically occur when clients record their dreams.

I often hear "I don't dream," or "If I do dream, I never remember them." Because dreams are stored in our short-term memory, they fade quickly when we wake up. Recording our dreams on waking, trains our subconscious mind that dreams are important, and we begin to remember dream fragments and eventually entire dreams. As we place more attention on our dreams, the more we will recall them.

Keeping a dream journal supports us in noticing patterns and recurring themes which can help us to connect ideas in new ways. This stimulates imagination and creativity which enhances our problem-solving capacities, creates new neural pathways, and opens our connection to universal consciousness. This gives us access to wisdom and intuition about the past, present and the future. Guidance from our universal self.

The practice is simple. Keep a notebook and pen on your night stand. The moment you wake up, write down whatever you remember from any dream you had. If you don't remember anything, simply write "Nothing remembered." Whether you recall a fragment or an entire dream, write down every detail in the sequence that they occurred, including the setting, characters, words spoken, and actions. Include details perceived through your senses, the colors, forms, temperature, sounds, smells and the feel of the surroundings.

Your Life Mission Statement

Creating your life mission or purpose statement from your Original Medicine will provide you a compass to evaluate decisions, a lens and filter through which to view your options. This helps to direct future actions so that you are moving forward in accordance with your true calling.

You must have solidified what a +10 feels like in your body. If not, go back to *Discerning "Yes" from "No"* in Chapter 3.

From the work you did earlier, mapping your peak moments, consider the common themes, core values, meaningful lessons, significant contributions, and complete the following statements:

• I'm at my best when I am

- I am being of service when I

_____

- I find enjoyment in my personal life through

_____

- _____ is the person / place / thing that brings me the most energy.

- I experience bliss when I_____ (place, activity)

- People tell me I'm good at:

_____

- When I _____,
I can lose track of time.

- I am in my element when _____, and

- I feel a deep connection with the people around me.

- I feel seen and accepted by these people:

_____

- I feel strangely drawn to (person, place or thing)

_____

- I enjoy work where I can

_____.

- I value _____ and will not sacrifice it, no matter what.

- I am using my natural talents and gifts when I

_____

- I can do anything I set my mind to, so I will

_____

- I want to be known for

_____

- My life's journey is about

_____

- I will be a person who _____ to
make a difference in the lives of others.

With a combination of what you've written above, write 1-3 sentences describing who you are at your best, and how you want your life to express that. Describe what it feels like when your universal self says "YES!!!" Keep reworking the words until it feels like YOUR Life Mission Statement. Post it in a place where you will see it and read it often, especially when you need a boost and to remind you of who you want to be and the impact you want to have on the world. When you value yourself, others will value you. Become so strong in the belief of what you're pursuing, others will see the value in it too.

Elderflower

Elder Trees are common in European mythology with a long history connected to ancient mysticism. There are rich legends of the Elder Tree being protective both psychically and physically. In Celtic fairie lore, the Elder held a place of respect for its ability to protect, to heal and to connect energies across worlds.

The berries and flowers are used in medicine. The flowers grow in bountiful creamy clusters and can be used in teas and baths to ease colds, flues, and hay fever.

Elderflower is beneficial as a diaphoretic; a hot infusion of the flowers induces sweating. Elder flower is indicated for viral infections accompanied by muscular aching, stiffness, rheumatic pain, and fever. The delicate, white flowers are also used to make syrups and cordials, such as the fruity liquor known as St. Germain.

Elder berries make delicious syrups and are an immune stimulant, containing antiviral phytochemicals.

In ancient times the spirit of this tree was referred to as the "Elder Mother." I consider Elderflower to be a powerful spiritual herb with the energy to awaken our intuition and induce vivid dreams. Drink a cup of tea before bedtime and have your Dream Journal and pen ready by the bed.

Sambucus nigra,
Elderflower

The prerequisite to accessing your personal power is the discovery of your Original Medicine. The moments that you activate it, you are dwelling in the magic of your destiny.

Chapter 6:

HOLD FAST TO YOUR THREAD

There's a thread you follow. It goes among
things that change. But it doesn't change.
People wonder about what you are pursuing.
You have to explain about the thread.
But it is hard for others to see.
While you hold it you can't get lost.
Tragedies happen; people get hurt
or die; and you suffer and get old.
Nothing you do can stop time's unfolding.
You don't ever let go of the thread.

— WILLIAM STAFFORD

You've found your thread. The thread that weaves from your universal self and through your life struggles and peak moments, interlacing the tapestry of your Original Medicine. It sparks your imagination and inspires your dreams. You hold fast to your thread as you traverse the terrain of life. It anchors you as you break free of your armor and question who you thought you were. You become the weaver of your own fate.

Our life tapestry is not limited by our past. Although it is a part of us, we continue to weave the patterns we want, adding unique colors and characteristics into the design of what our life is becoming. As the weaver, we are the creator, choosing to use our thread in distinctive and artistic ways.

At about this time in the process, I see a common theme begin to surface with clients. The fear of failure. Often the fear is of a financial nature. If we take the risk of putting ourselves out there and then fail, we might lose everything and become destitute. Or worse we fear that failure will prove once and for all that we really aren't worthy of success or happiness, or wealth. So, we avoid failure like the plague and live in constant fear of it.

Our culture teaches us that the Universe is a hostile place where multiple things are trying to hurt us. So, we live in a cage of our own creation, grasping and clinging to safety. Albert Einstein said, "The most important decision we make is whether we believe we live in a friendly or hostile universe." Our work is to become aware of what is frightening us and how we pull back from it. Then developing a resilience to tolerating the discomfort. Allowing it to just be. Sitting with it. Not moving away from it because given the space and time, it will move itself.

Lizard Fears

The human brain is anatomically made up of three different neural structures that developed successively during evolution: The reptilian brain or brain stem is the oldest of the three and controls the body's vital functions (heart rate, breathing, body temperature.) Our reptilian brain tends to be rigid and compulsive. The limbic brain, sometimes referred to as the mammalian brain in human beings, is responsible for emotions, memories and habits. It makes value judgements that influence our behavior. The third structure is the neocortex or the higher brain which is responsible for communication, creativity, abstract thought, imagination and consciousness.

The reptilian brain doesn't recognize time, so it doesn't know that you are no longer a child. Therefore, we can get triggered as adults and react the same way we did as children. It literally takes a millisecond for our brainstem to react to a stimulus and create a fear response designed to protect us and ensure our survival. This is a great system when we are dealing with a real threat to our safety. The problem is when the fear is triggered by an imaginary or perceived threat. This is typically the case when we aren't putting ourselves out there because of the fear of failure. Unfortunately, as important as it is that our reptilian brain is trying to protect us, we tend to listen to it far too much, which causes fear, worry, anxiety, stress, and ultimately suffering. The more we worry and think fear-filled thoughts, the more sensitized this part of our brain becomes. Our thoughts, and the stories our minds fabricate, produce an emotional feedback loop that creates more fear.

Unconsciously responding to automatic reptilian fear

responses without awareness, blocks us from making choices in support of our growth, creativity, and unique genius. One of those unconscious responses is often around money. Studies have shown that because of our distorted relationship with money, 3 out of 4 Americans identify money as the number one source of stress in their lives.

Money is a touchy subject for most people. We develop attitudes and beliefs about money in childhood. This means that depending on how we were raised to think about money, we can easily get triggered into fear around finances. From a childhood of poverty to subconscious messages from parents, there are so many ways we can develop a distorted relationship with money.

We all live according to who we believe we are. We define ourselves in our youth–we make choices about what we can and can't do, what to believe, what we are capable of, who we are. We established a set of standards and beliefs that become the box we keep ourselves in and at some point, we accepted those limitations. "That's who I am." "That's how it is." This is particularly evident when it comes to financial status and worthiness around income.

Time and time again, I hear from women about their fear around money. What is fascinating is how seldom money or the lack of it, is the real issue. Rather, it is the fear of lack of money that the reptilian brain is hardwired around that it is preventing forward movement. These are "What if" future-fretting fears about the lack of money.

Once we understand how and why our reptilian brain gets stimulated, and the choices we make because of it and what we tend to avoid, to not feel the fear, we can begin distancing ourselves from it. Unless you are under eminent danger, survival fears are almost always harmless. Fear is a very good thing when it is telling us that something is a threat to our wellbeing. We need to distinguish real fear from false fear, often a cover for anxiety or worry. False fear paralyzes us and keeps us from acting. Real fear is instinctive, and we must act on it.

Tracking Your Reptilian Brain

See if you can identify your most common false fears. In your journal, complete the following sentences:

1. I don't have enough _____
2. No one cares about me because _____
3. If I don't watch out, someone will _____
4. I can't be perfectly happy until I get _____
5. I just can't trust _____
6. People will hurt me unless _____
7. If only I had _____
8. I must hang on to _____
9. I'll never be able to _____
10. I will lose everything if I _____
11. I don't deserve _____

Are you able to see a trend about what thoughts are causing your fears? Remember, unless you are actually in danger, your reptilian brain is conjuring up the thoughts that are leading to the way you feel.

Make a list of the feelings that arise when you believe that any of these statements is true. Do you feel anxious or exhausted or sad or hopeless?

Now write down what you typically choose to do when you feel that way. Do you want to eat an entire pint of ice cream, or get on the computer, or go back to bed? Just notice without judgement. This is all about increasing your awareness of how you might be blocking your own success and happiness. The most powerful way to get out of the cage of safety is through peace. Come into the present moment of now and find peace for even just a few moments. "Right now, in this moment, I'm okay." Just breathe in a sense of peace. That place of peace will be the platform to create what you desire more than you could ever create from a place of fear. Release your attachment for anything to be different than it is. When we brace or tighten around fear we give it more power. Acknowledge it and allow it and it will soften and change shape. Resisting it will make it get louder.

"I resist nothing."

"I allow my feelings to be as they are."

"I allow my fear to be as it is."

"I let go of all resistance."

"I see you fear, I feel you and acknowledge you."

Fear is not the foundation to building abundance. Our willingness to feel our emotions, including fear, allows them to shift and change. This openness creates a benevolent space for what wants to happen.

I started working with a business owner about a

year after she launched a new product line for families. She couldn't understand why she wasn't able to sell her products, even though she knew she had created something special that would help make life easier for parents with young children. We identified the ideal sales channels for her product line which was helpful. But what really made the lightbulb light up in her head was when she discovered that every time she began to create a sales strategy, make a sales call or think about hiring a sales person, she would become paralyzed with fear. To avoid it, she would go back to her website and spend hours making tweaks and avoid what felt hard. As if it was the gospel truth, she believed this recurring reptilian thought: "I'll never be able to know enough to run this business successfully." Questioning this belief created space from it so she could make some sales calls and set up appointments to show her line to a few retail chain buyers. Within a few months, she had made $80,000 in sales.

Examine the worrisome, scary, and painful thoughts that habitually occupy your mind. Ask yourself if this is what you want to drive the way you feel and react. If the answer is no, become the wise one and tell your reptilian brain: "It's okay, I've got this. I can do this and even if I fail, it will be okay." Don't let your brain stop you before you even start. Once you know your fear-inducing thoughts, the next step is noticing them as they pop up. If you feel a negative sensation in your body, trace your thoughts back to what might have caused it.

To create awareness around your thoughts, start by using this tool from Acceptance and Commitment Therapy. Whenever you notice yourself caught up in thoughts like the ones you wrote about above, say to yourself: "I notice I'm thinking... [insert thought here.]"

This may seem too simple to be effective, but it's actually one of the most powerful ways to start making different choices. By repeatedly noticing your thinking, instead of allowing yourself to habitually react to it, you slowly create the ability to see beyond the thoughts that are causing you to feel overwhelmed, insecure, scared, and anxious. Your universal self can then make the choices aligned with what feels right in that moment. Doing this relaxes the control our mind has over us, guiding us towards our inner wisdom. This is our true course. "The mind is a wonderful servant, but a terrible master."

Remember the mind-body connection from Chapter 2? Choosing a thought that creates more ease, relaxation and expansion in your body is a choice you have in every moment of every day. Peaceful thoughts create peaceful actions. You may still have fearful thoughts, however with awareness, you can question them before they cause suffering feelings and block you from making a different choice. Fear is a universal reality for innovators who are creating change and living in their truth. It's only an issue when it stops us from doing our work in the world. Feeling fear, reassuring our reptilian brain that "I've got this!" and breathing into it, is an incredibly powerful and motivating force.

In *Big Magic,* Elizabeth Gilbert says: "Dearest Fear: Creativity and I are about to go on a road trip. I understand you'll be joining us, because you always do. I acknowledge that you believe you have an important job to do. But I will also be doing my job, which is to work hard and stay focused. And Creativity will be doing its job, which is to remain stimulating and inspiring. There's plenty of room in this vehicle for all of us but understand this: Creativity and I are the only ones who will be making any decisions along the way. You're not allowed to suggest detours. You're not allowed to fiddle with the temperature. Dude, you're not even allowed to touch the radio. But above all else, you are absolutely forbidden to drive."

Fear and excitement are the same sensation in the body and the same neurotransmitters in the brain. We may feel excitement, but the mind reads it as fear. Move toward love, not away from fear. Allow fear, sit with it, don't move. It will move itself.

Take a Vacation from Concern

We need time to reflect, to step back, and ask ourselves why we do what we do. Self-care and time for reflection are crucial for anyone trying to do anything meaningful in life, like running a business, raising children, trying to launch a start-up, or nurturing a relationship. This is especially true if you are navigating a life transition. Self-care is essential to have the capacity to hold fast to your thread.

Accept and love the part of you that is worried and concerned, begging for your love and approval. There is no part of you that is wrong, only the part of you that needs to be loved more. It's not that your concerns are imaginary, it's that worry is not going to resolve them.

When we accept the one in us who worries and is fueled by concern, we aren't trying to change ourselves we are just offering ourselves love, support, companionship, and compassion. "For as long as you're concerned for however long you choose to worry, I will be your faithful, dedicated companion, who listens to your concerns, feels your fears, and holds you. I love you."

When we comfort the part of us that is concerned, we allow the space within ourselves for inspiration to be unleashed. Nothing is a distraction from being our most powerful selves. What I have observed in my work is a common belief that goes something like: "If I'm not concerned then I'm not going to be helpful with what the world needs of me." Being concerned takes up so much time and energy that we aren't being effective in action. When we are unconcerned, we have nothing distracting us. When we're concerned, we're so paralyzed by worries that we can't be effective.

To put concern aside, start with a self-love practice. Finding your true self requires rest, being in the presence of NOW and just being okay for a few moments without the mind as the controller. Giving yourself a break from concern is the first step, a break from the stream of thoughts in your head. Then as you feel a softening inside, ask yourself a series of questions:

- Is there a part of me, a felt something inside of me that isn't concerned?

- In the background behind that part, is there a voice saying, "I should be concerned"?

- Can I give myself permission to not feel concerned?

- Who am I without my concern?

The part of you that isn't concerned is the truth.

I had a client several years ago so immobilized by worry that she could barely leave her condo. She was worried about her kids, she was worried about how people would view her now that she was divorced, she was worried about her financial future, and she worried about the state of the world. She fretted her way through every day. When she started giving herself the love and comfort she was craving, she took a vacation from concern, and could engage with life. She began with an outing to the bookstore to pick up a good book to read. The more she relaxed, the greater her capacity to start new things. When she dared to be unconcerned for a moment, she could see and feel differently. This is the only way we can foster deep spiritual exploration. Presence is a state of being unconcerned. Spiritual exploration begins here. When we allow the body to let go of tension, we can relax and find stillness and calm. Then we are open to the gentle sensations of inner wisdom.

Doing the Scary Thing

We have all found ourselves in situations that feel impossible and may even be unhealthy, we feel stuck and afraid, yet we cannot see a way out. There is often one critical step that might change everything. However, to take this step requires an act of courage. It's the thing you believe you could never do.

If this is the way you are feeling right now, know that you are NOT alone. After 27 years of coaching, these are the ways I have seen clients get stuck –

- A toxic or abusive relationship where you are hiding to keep the peace
- A career that feels miserable
- Stress that leads to drinking (or eating) to relieve the pressure
- High levels of anxiety and worry about the welfare of loved ones
- Feeling overwhelmed yet not asking for help
- Exhausted trying to make everyone else happy
- Questioning your self-worth and feeling insecure
- Feeling bullied, undervalued or controlled

I recently worked with a client who was involved in an emotionally depleting and verbally abusive relationship. I listened to the painful story of how she progressively lost herself a little bit more every day until after 10 years, she felt like a shell of her former self. For years, decades even, she kept her feelings and needs bottled up inside to avoid a reaction or conflict. She believed that by hiding her true feelings she was keeping the marriage more harmonious and intact. By ignoring her needs and suppressing her voice, she was unwittingly giving away her power.

Learning to allow fear and to harness the energy of it, is a critical tool in the world we live in. I used to avoid feeling fear; I would do anything to run away from it, usually by getting busy doing something, as a distraction. I believed that if I accomplished something, I would squelch the fear; productivity would make me feel good and then the fear would go away on its own. Fear that isn't felt and faced, remains in the body and can cause stress, ill health and pain.

I see fear as a blessing. **Fear is just the energetic preparation for something that is important to do.** Fear can even be harnessed and used to increase confidence. Fear can pull us out of our thoughts and become a pathway into our body.

If you feel inspired to be more courageous at home, at work, with your children, with your partner, and you want to show up and be seen, turn your fear into courage.

The first step is avoiding distractions. Stop doing; stop eating (or drinking,) and stop distracting yourself from the fear. Before you reach for the door handle on the refrigerator, stop, take a breath and ask, "Am I hungry or am I feeling a difficult emotion?" If you aren't hungry, sit down and practice the next step. Do the same thing if you find yourself looking for what else you need to get done. My old pattern was to check my To Do list to see what I needed to get done. Pause between each task and just feel.

The next step is to feel the fear. Create a regular practice of quieting the mind. Notice the sensation of your breath coming in and out of your body. Really feel your breath expand into your lungs and abdomen, then out through your nose or mouth. As you feel your breath, notice how it expands beyond your torso into every cell of your body. If you get distracted at any point, bring your attention back to your breath and body. Bring your attention deeper inside to your inner body. Now notice any fear or anxiety. Notice where you are feeling it in your body. Just ALLOW it. Don't panic and run away from it by allowing your mind to get distracted. Keep your attention on it while breathing until the fear starts to expand. It might start to feel like it is getting softer and yet larger in size, almost like steam as it billows and dissipates. Sit with this until you feel a sense of deep calm and peace. This is your universal self and the part of you that can create whatever your soul desires. This is courage.

If you know it's time to make a life change and the thought of it grips you with fear, write down your goals. Thucydides, a Greek philosopher during the 5th Century, B.C., said "The bravest are surely those who have the clearest vision of what is before them, glory and danger alike, and yet notwithstanding, go out to meet it." Do you have a vision for your future? It is critical to set your goals from a place of heart or love. When you think about your goal, does it feel joyful and fun? Does it come from a place of love rather than fear? When you imagine your ideal life, ideal relationship, ideal career, what do you see? Write down what it feels like. What is a reasonable timeframe for you to get there? Once you have a goal in mind, working backwards, break it down into small steps that will get you from where you are now to the goal. Small, doable steps will boost your courage to move forward. Using the energy of fear to move you into action is what creates courage. What is the smallest first step you can take today? I tell my clients to find a step that it is so ridiculously easy; it would be absurd not to do it. If the step feels too daunting, break it down further. Chapter 7 will define this in greater detail.

Reach out for support. Make a list of the friends and family you know who can provide the emotional support and encouragement for you to take that first courageous step. Who can you call and talk about what is scary for you? Who is your tribe? Deliberately surround yourself with people who inspire you and believe in you. Ask for help in taking that one critical step that will change everything. Being vulnerable in relationships creates deeper connection and inspires others to be vulnerable and courageous also. I keep a list very near to me of my support team and on days when it feels like life is too much for me to handle alone, I reach out. Getting support is a self-loving act.

Building our courage muscle means first and foremost being compassionate with ourselves. When we critique and belittle ourselves in our thoughts, we keep ourselves small. Doing something brave requires that we trust ourselves. Self-encouragement is critical to being courageous. What is the most self-loving thing you can do right now? Start with self-care—feeling safe is #1; getting enough sleep and eating healthfully. What makes you happy? Being in nature, getting a hug, spending time with loved ones and pets, singing, dancing, and writing? Make the time to do something that is just for you. Spend your precious time doing the things that you love to do. When I need a lift, I go outside and commune with my hummingbird buddy (yes, I have one!) and the flowers in my garden.

Acknowledge and celebrate how you are bravely showing up in your life—every small or large accomplishment, as well as your mistakes. Failures mean that you are putting yourself out there! Failure is essential to success. The most significant accomplishments arise out of failures. So, whether you are posting your artwork online, telling a friend the truth of how you feel even though they may get angry or hurt, raising your hand to speak up in meetings, expressing your needs to your partner, showing your kids that you value yourself enough to take time for you… these are acts of bravery and will strengthen your courage muscle.

As we explored in Chapter 3, saying "no" to others

often means saying, "yes" to ourselves. If you think that you're being a good person each time you say "yes," think again. Each time you agree to something that doesn't feel good in your gut, you are giving away a little bit more of your power. Notice all the places in your life that you aren't saying yes to yourself. Turn anything that feels like "I should" into "I choose to." Everywhere you choose to give your energy and time, consider if it is in alignment with what is most important to you. Are you doing it for approval? The only person you need to receive approval from is you. Using discernment in where you choose to give of your energy is living your truth. This is honesty. Saying no to others when you need to prioritize your own needs is an act of courage. Tasks become pleasing, done with love rather than resentment. After years of taking care of everything and everyone else before herself, the client who stuffed her own needs and feelings now makes her own health and happiness the highest priority. And her marriage is better because of it.

Fear never goes away, we just learn how to use it.

> *Here's what is truly at the heart of whole-heartedness: Worthy Now. Not if. Not when. We are worthy of love and belonging now. Right this minute. As is. There are no prerequisites to "I am enough".*

> —Brené Brown

Find the freedom that comes from harnessing your courage and believe that you are enough exactly as you are. What you feel and need are valid. Welcome fear as the catalyst and motivator to do what is difficult and essential for you to do.

Purify Your Vessel

Because the body is our barometer for the soul, our built-in navigation system, to hear the whisperings of our inner wisdom, we must keep the barometer as clear as possible. Purifying the vessel that speaks our wisdom and breaking free of protective armor are the work we must do. Keeping the physical body clean prepares it for acting as the guidance that our universal selves need to navigate through life. Every religion teaches about purification of the body for empowering the senses and attaining spiritual development. Buddha taught that to be purified enables one to merge with the truth within.

My simple recommendations for keeping the vessel clear:

- Start the day with fresh lemon water to flush out toxins and alkalize the body. (This is great to do just before meditating!)

- Drink a fresh squeezed juice every day with plenty of greens like kale and spinach with apples, carrots, and fresh ginger

- Eat healthy oils like olive, coconut, avocado, hemp, and flaxseed

- Eat plenty of raw fruits and vegetables for the enzymes that help with digestion and absorption
- Drink herbal tea; the suggestions provided in this book are highly recommended
- Minimize the consumption of sugar and artificial sweeteners
- Take probiotics
- Eat more legumes and less meat
- Get outside, breathe deeply and find the blessings in every day

I've talked several times about breaking free of the protective armor we developed in childhood. As adults, armor prevents us from being in touch with the wisdom within that is communicated through the gentle sensations in our bodies. The body is the pathway into our calling. Disassociation from our body disconnects us from that process.

To shed the armor, we must practice being vulnerable. We may have learned early on that being vulnerable is dangerous and can cause us to get hurt. However, we must risk being socially exposed to be true to ourselves. This requires showing up and being seen instead of staying safe. It means braving criticism and being hurt to live fully into our destiny. This is particularly challenging for women with a good girl tendency.

Our real work is about revealing ourselves as we truly are, not just on the outside but on the inside. The parts of us that are messy and broken. We must start putting our work out in the world regardless of how imperfect we might think it is. We'll screw up and that's okay—actually, that's awesome. It's awesome because it gives us the opportunity to feel vulnerable while also seeing that the world didn't end because of it. This is how we build courage and get rid of the armor and the perfectionism that are the obstacles to living our true calling. Don't allow your scars to act as tough, resistant guards against future damage. Crisis shapes us, leaving us wiser, deeper, and more connected to what really matters to us.

I have come to understand that women and men undertake plans in very different ways. Women must move forward from a felt inner experience, allowing inner wisdom and intuition to propel forward movement. Whereas men tend to work from the outside in, setting future goals and then breaking those goals down into steps, women work from the inside out, feeling a desire in the body first and then following that inner guidance towards the next step, then the next step after that. To hear that inner guidance, we must:

- Shed the armor by allowing ourselves to be vulnerable
- Take care of our navigational system so the directional information is clear
- Let go of concern and tension to be able access inner calm so that we can perceive what is waiting to be heard
- Develop trust in the guidance by using it as the basis for life choices

Tools and Exercises

Personal Love Statement

In 2016, Matt Kahn released his new book, *Whatever Arises, Love That*, which instantly became my new favorite spiritual book. What I love about Matt's profound message, is that we can move from victimhood to empowerment in one moment. I get goosebumps ("truth" bumps) in response to profound truth and boy did I get them when I read Matt's message about how a love revolution begins with each of us. That we are the one we've been waiting for. If you've been waiting your whole life to hear someone say that you are loved, that you are worthy, you need not wait another moment.

Think of anyone who has hurt you or had a deep effect on your feelings of self-worth. What do you wish they had said to you?

What are the words you didn't hear enough of?

That is the exact thing you begin saying to yourself. Your Personal Love Statement.

You've been waiting for someone else to say this, but you no longer need to wait. You can become the one to tell you the words you've always wanted to hear and, in this way, you begin to heal yourself from the inside out.

Some of the statements that clients have created:

- You are safe
- I love you
- I always want to hear what you have to say

- You are beautiful
- You were wanted
- There's an important reason you are here
- You can do no wrong

A simple practice for implementing your Personal Love Statement is to stand in front of a mirror, look into your eyes say your Personal Love Statement out loud. To yourself. Every day. Three times each day.

When I suggest my clients try this, they're amazed how much resistance comes up for them. They are so accustomed to believing the lies they tell themselves every day. Speak the truth to yourself. Remember what Eben Alexander heard repeatedly during his near-death experience:

You are loved and cherished, dearly and forever.
You have nothing to fear.
There is nothing you can do wrong.

It's time to give yourself the love that you've been waiting for. Be your own beloved. We must do the healing which is ours to heal. When we take care of ourselves, we take care of the world. As we midwife our own healing, in the process we develop such a way that we can midwife the healing of another. We can make others feel good simply because we have a healing quality.

Love the one in you who is sad and scared and angry and lonely. Love the part of you who hates herself. When we love all of the ones we are, we will know how to love each other and the world.

Your Ideal Day Visualization

(Download the mp3 audio guide for this visualization at: www.rootedinpurpose.com)

You are going to take a leisurely walk through a day that would be the very substance of your life as you'd love it to be. You will live through that future day in the present tense and *in detail*, from getting up in the morning to going to sleep at night.

Find a spot where you can sit for 15 minutes without being interrupted. Let's begin by relaxing. Finding our inner peace is the groundwork for rooting into creativity, inspiration and imagination. Find a comfortable chair and sit down or lie down if you are in a place where you can do that. If you're sitting, uncross your legs. Get as relaxed as you possibly can and take a few deep breaths. Our bodies associate long, deep, slow breaths with relaxation. By consciously taking long exhales and then full inhales, we are showing our bodies that we feel safe enough to let go. If you are in a place where you can close your eyes, please do that. Now feel your feet on the ground. Feel what the fabric of your socks feels like if you're wearing them. Feel your feet in your shoes, feel the floor underneath your feet.

Take a few unusually long breaths, inhaling through your nose and exhaling through your mouth. Notice with each in-breath, your belly fills up like a balloon and with each exhale, you feel tension release and feel your muscles melt into the chair. Now bring your attention to the base of your spine. Imagine that with each breath, you're growing a root down into the Earth. Feel your root go through the floor, then further into the rich dark soil that covers the planet. Feel the cool of the soil as you go deeper, moving away from sunlight and air. With each breath, grow your root deeper and deeper, through clear, underground springs and rock, all the way to the heart of the planet. Sit for a moment and bask in your deep connection to the Earth.

Now with each breath, draw up energy from the Earth's center. See the energy rise through the Earth's layers, slowly with each breath until it reaches the base of your spine. Begin breathing normally and notice the rise and fall of your chest.

In your mind's eye, imagine a time about 5 years from now. How old will you be? How old will your children be? This is your best life, one in which you have no unmet needs and no fear. This is a typical day in your ideal life. Not a special day, not a holiday or your birthday, just an everyday day, but exactly as you would like it to be. An average day in your perfect life. You are enjoying close and heart-connected relationships. You have many beings in your life who adore you and you adore. There may be a partner, friends, coworkers, teammates, children, and animals in your life. Take a deep breath in, hold it at the apex for the count of three as completely empty out your lungs as you release it. With your next exhale, you're going to wake up in your ideal day.

Without opening your eyes, I want you to wake up refreshed and notice what you can hear. Listen to the sounds wherever you are, in the room, in the house, outside. Can you hear the ocean? A cat? Traffic? Wind?

Smell the air. Can you smell breakfast cooking? The smell of the ocean? Pine trees? Notice the temperature and the movement of air. What can you feel on your skin? What do the sheets feel like? What does the air feel like on your skin? Can you tell what season it is?

Open your eyes and look around. What is the space like? What does your bedroom look like? Look at the surroundings—the windows, walls. What colors do you see? Is there art on the walls? What can you see outside the window? Are you in an apartment in Manhattan? A cabin in the woods? Do you see a clock or a calendar? If so, what day or time is it? Are there photographs from the last five years? Is there someone next to you?

Get up and stretch and start walking through your day.

Go into the bathroom. What does it look like? Look at yourself in a full-length mirror. This is your ideal life. Your body is your ideal body—perfect fitness and weight. Enjoy how good you look and feel.

Go to your closet and notice the clothes and shoes you need for your ideal life. What kind of clothes do you have? Do you have gowns, overalls, business suits, fancy dresses? Look at your shoes. Do you have mud boots, running shoes, flats, heels, ballet shoes? Put on an outfit that is perfectly comfy and perfectly beautiful and perfectly suited to your ideal lifestyle.

Now you are ready for your day. You are going to do something that makes you very happy! You feel motivated and can't wait to get to it.

Go have breakfast. Walk through your living space, through your kitchen and eat a delicious breakfast with your favorite people. What are you having for breakfast? Do you make it yourself or was it prepared for you?

Take a virtual tour of your house. Notice the quality, tone and feel of the atmosphere. In what kind of place, space, situation do you live? An apartment, a farmhouse, a workshop, an elegant hotel room, a houseboat?

Who else is there? Notice the love of each individual and how it feels to be seen and heard.

Now you'll begin your work. This is the real work of your life. Your soul's preferred occupation. Your life's calling. Go to the place that you work. Where do you go during the day? What do you do for work? What does your work space or office look like? Are you outside or indoors? Are you alone or are other people there? Are you working together? Notice yourself doing your work. You are completely immersed in the process. Without thinking or forcing notice what your real life's work feels like. Are you connecting with people or material objects, machines, with ideas? Are you working with people and organizations? Are you moving or holding still? What does the area or room look like? What do you see, hear and touch and feel as you do your work? What kind of problems are solving? Notice any specific images or sensations that come up without labeling them.

Proceed through the natural course of your day as you conduct the work of your ideal life. How do you spend the morning? Break for lunch. Notice where you go for lunch, who you go with and what you eat.

Go to what you do in the afternoon. Is it at work or something different? Spend your afternoon exactly as you wish at work or play, socializing, caregiving or adventuring. As you go through the hours of your day, be aware of what you are doing, where you are and with who. If you'd like to play a musical instrument or sail, in your ideal day, you know how.

When you finish your work day, where do you go next? Are you preparing dinner or is someone else? Who are you sharing your dinner table with? Notice the feeling of each loving individual and the wonderful dinner conversation. Spend the evening doing whatever you enjoy doing in your free time. Who do you eat with, laugh, talk and sleep with?

Go to bed feeling pleasantly and perfectly tired. Before you go to sleep, take a deep breath and ground the feelings of your ideal day into the center of your being.

When you're ready, take a deep breath, and as you exhale anchor the feelings of the visualization as you move toward this ideal day becoming a reality. Open your eyes.

In your journal, write down all the details from your visualization, including how you felt both emotionally and bodily sensations.

Vision Board

After you've written the details from your guided visualization in your journal, it's helpful to create a visual collage of the images that came up during the visualization. Creating a visual representation of what we are seeking, naturally guides our attention there.

You'll need:

- A piece of poster board (or you can also use the cover of your journal)
- Glue
- Magazines and old calendars
- Scissors
- Stickers, colored paper and other scrapbooking materials are great but not essential

Now you are ready to create your collage. This experience is powerful to do after your Ideal Day Visualization while the images are still fresh in your mind. It's important that you create from your universal self, not your societal self. Your societal self might select images that reflect the "I shoulds" and "I have tos" rather than visioning from your Original Medicine. This is about creating a collection of images that represent an imagined future.

Sit somewhere comfortable with a cup of tea. Create a sacred space by lighting a candle. Relax, breathing deeply and feel your way through as you leaf through the magazines and select images and words that resonate with your body. You don't need to find ideal images, there is no perfect way to create a vision board. Just tear out images and words that call out to you as you pour through the magazines. Notice when images create body sensations that feel good. This might feel like a feel of relaxation in your head or a feeling of lightness or expansion in your chest. Try not to get pulled into the marketing or spend too much time on each page.

Cut and glue the images and words you've torn out on to your poster board in any way that inspires you. The images don't need to go together in any way aside from being pleasing to you. You are assembling pictures and words that appeal to your universal self and spark your imagination. The process of creating this visual representation of what your universal self is seeking will steer your subconscious and conscious choices.

When you feel complete with your vision board, put it in a place where you will see it often. Clients have found it effective to take a picture of their vision board and use it as the wallpaper on their smart phone or laptop. Having opportunities where you can be regularly reminded of your future self is motivating and inspirational.

Motherwort

Motherwort is my favorite calmative herb for easing heartache, especially related to painful life memories. There's a reason the species name is *cardiaca*. It lifts sadness and brings brightness to the heart. Because of its profound effect on the nervous system, Motherwort soothes and comforts irritated nervous, stress, tension, and anxiety. The genus name *Leonurus*, Latin for "lion" (*Leonurus cardiaca* means "lion-hearted") is telling in Motherwort's ability to embolden courage during times when additional reserve is needed.

Although it is a member of the mint family, Motherwort is bitter, so I don't recommend it as an herbal tea. Motherwort herbal vinegar is rich in calcium and antioxidants. Fill a jar with fresh Motherwort leaves (it grows easily in the garden) and cover with apple cider vinegar, leaving ½"of air at the top of the jar. Place a piece of wax paper of the top before you screw on the lid. Place in the kitchen cupboard for 6 weeks, shaking it from time to time. You can use this nutritive, restorative, relaxing vinegar in soups, dressings, juice or take it by the tablespoon.

Leonurus cardiaca, Motherwort

We build courage and confidence by stepping out of our comfort zone and doing what feels scary. If it feels a little scary, then it must be important to do.

Chapter 7:
YOUR ROOTS IN
THE GROUND

In out-of-the-way places of the heart,
Where your thoughts never think to wander,
This beginning has been quietly forming,
Waiting until you were ready to emerge.
For a long time, it has watched your desire,
Feeling the emptiness growing inside you,
Noticing how you willed yourself on,
Still unable to leave what you had outgrown.
It watched you play with the seduction of safety
And the gray promises that sameness whispered,
Heard the waves of turmoil rise and relent,
Wondered would you always live like this.
Then the delight, when your courage kindled,
And out you stepped onto new ground,
Your eyes young again with energy and dream,
A path of plenitude opening before you.
Though your destination is not yet clear
You can trust the promise of this opening;
Unfurl yourself into the grace of beginning
That is at one with your life's desire.
Awaken your spirit to adventure;

Hold nothing back, learn to find ease in risk;
Soon you will be home in a new rhythm,
For your soul senses the world that awaits you.

— John O'Donohue

By this point, you've begun important self-work and no doubt have some new and interesting perspectives about yourself. Congratulations on your willingness to go deep and feel your vulnerability. If you've followed the flow of the journey, you have:

- Reconnected with your universal self through body awareness

- Dissolved the limiting thoughts and beliefs that have been holding you back and keeping you small

- Touched into your Original Medicine and picked up your thread

- Created awareness around fear and how to calm down your reptilian brain

- Taken steps towards greater self-love and self-care

- Begun the shedding of your armor

- Opened to clear inner guidance

- Tapped into your imagination and accessed visual images as well as the felt sense of what your universal self is wanting to create

Our life callings should fulfill three needs, 1) Pay the bills (this is something you have to do, 2) Serve the world or involve a cause, 3) Frighten you just enough to push you beyond your comfort zone and keep life interesting.

Ideal into Real

Now it's time to begin the practical work of moving from ideal into real. Whatever we create must be born from the energy of peace. How do you know you are creating from that place? You can feel it in your body. We can't create our life's calling from shallow, fear-based energy. When we create from a place of peace, we are in alignment with our soul's purpose.

One thing I should mention at this point is that turning your dream into reality isn't easy. However, it's essential to remember the process of struggle is critical to the outcome. We gain strength from trying and failing. Each time we fail, it gives us an opportunity to dissolve a limiting belief and reclaim our commitment to self-care. When we are at the edge of doing something that feels a bit hard, we access our inner fortitude and hence find deeper meaning in the process.

I have observed clients at this stage, exuberant in their newfound connection with their inner wisdom, and passionate about what they want to pursue. They jump in feet first and take steps that are too big. Inevitably they have a setback which slams them back into their limiting beliefs and triggers defeat. This can result in giving up.

Take small steps! The teeniest steps you can take. One at a time. Little by little. Expect to fail. The smaller the steps, the lesser the mistakes. As you make progress, and become more knowledgeable and more confident, the steps can get bigger. But start small.

We are going to explore three tools to move from ideal into real.

1. Alternative Lives
2. Plausibility Exploration
3. Working Your Timeline Backwards

Tools and Exercises

Alternative Lives

As you worked through the exercises of tracking your peak moments, conjuring up your imagination and writing your Life Mission Statement, you have a hold of your thread and a sense of your innate gifts. Now we will move from into the forming of life callings from these gifts

For many people, there are multiple options that call out to them. When you created your Life Mission Statement, what impact did you want to have on the world?

500 Lives

Answer this question in your journal.

Regardless of your religious beliefs, pretend you have 500 lives to live sequentially here on Earth. What's more, you get to remember each of your lives as you begin the next one. Anything you start right now in this life, you have hundreds of years to tweak and reform and work on it to get it right. (A rough calculation means this would be 4,500 years, 2,000 kids, 500 jobs.) What is one thing you want to have accomplished by the time you finish your 500[th]life?

Innovate Three Real Life Alternatives.

Allow at least forty-five minutes for this exercise.

Let's play with different jobs, business endeavors, volunteering ideas, and career options.

1. Grab your journal (again!)

2. You have three life options. Whichever one you end up choosing, it must be completed within the next five years of your life. I have found that five years isn't too short or too long. For each one, write in as much detail as possible. Write about three possible variations of your next five years:

   Life One: This option is centered on what you already have in mind that you thought you should do or wanted to do. This option may be what you are current doing, expanded forward or it might be the inspired fresh idea that you've been nurturing forward.

   Life Two: This option is what would do if the Life One option were suddenly gone and no longer available. This has happened. For example, if you were thinking you wanted to open a video rental store yet that wasn't an option because renting movies is becoming obsolete. What would you do? Think about how you would make a living doing something other than the Life One option.

Life Three: This option is the thing you would do or the life you'd live if money or image were no object. You would do this if you knew no one would laugh at you or think less of you for doing it. This option should be a little bit wild, far-fetched, and crazy.

3. Create a six-word title for each of the options

4. When you've completed writing about all three of your alternative life options, go for a walk, take a bath, sit outside with a cup of tea and watch what percolates.

5. Spend ten minutes writing in your journal.

I relish hearing what clients create in this process. Everything from writing a fantasy novel, being a yoga teacher, and sailing around the globe, to opening an animal sanctuary, leading spiritual retreats and being a priestess healer. There is nothing that isn't possible! Truly. I have celebrated clients in the creation of nearly every one of their dreams become a reality.

Plausibility Exploration

To assess the plausibility of your three life options, you need to collect data about each of them. The simplest way to collect data is by asking questions and having conversations with someone who is already doing what you're thinking of or has expertise in that option. If you have a life option in mind that you really don't know much about, interviewing someone in that industry is immensely helpful. Perhaps you're interested in being a journalist, ask within your network for help in finding a reporter that you could take to coffee. Most people love talking about their work. Another way to collect data is to design an actual experience of the life option that will allow you to try it out, even if for just an hour or a day. Shadow that reporter for a day to get first hand familiarity with their job.

Researching your alternative lives gives you the opportunity to meet people involved in that type of work, including influencers in the field and begin to develop a community of support. Experiential research allows you to try out that life option without having invested a lot of resources. On more than one occasion, I've heard incredible stories about how this research process has led to unexpected opportunities. We human beings generally want to help each other. Someone connects you to a friend or colleague, one conversation leads to another and before you know it you have developed a network of people who are supporting your goal and working on your behalf.

1. For all three of your life options:
    a. Tap into body awareness. Sit with each option and discern how it registers in your body, on a scale from -10 to +10 (Chapter 3)

b. Rate the coherence of each option against your Life Mission Statement (Chapter 5)

c. Come up with three questions for what you would want to investigate, test and explore about each alternative. For example, what is the geographic requirement, experience necessary, and the impacts on family? Questions should be focused on what your daily life will look like, training you might need, and how you will need to adjust your current situation.

d. Now, for each life option, gauge the resources that will be required, i.e. time, money, education, skill, contacts.

Remember how the process of struggle is critical to the outcome? This step of your creativity allows you to try and fail. The most challenging sought victories require us to reach deep inside and access our resources. In the process, we gain a deeper understanding of our imitations and strengths. Life's failures, defeats and complete wipeouts are our greatest teachers and when we accept them as the learning opportunities that they are without self-recrimination, when we get up and try again, we build our courage muscle and our belief in ourselves. Life offers us invitations to separate from parts of ourselves and shift into who we are destined to become. Where are the parts of you that are melting away and no longer serving your highest good?

Failures aren't truly "failures." They are the essential

cracks in the shells of our identities. They are the vital breakings of our hearts along the passageway of life that alter the way we see ourselves and the world. Everything we view as a mistake is just an education.

One day you will wake up and decide what you want to do. A thought will come up to do something you've never done before. Get out and do it woman! Be brave. Fail often.

2. Now that you've assessed each life option and come up with your research questions, it's time to make a list of any contacts you have that could connect you with someone in the industry for a conversation. Someone who is either doing or living what you are considering. I encourage clients to view this as getting someone's story. The story of how that person got to be doing that thing and what it's really like to do what she does. What training or experience did she need? What does a typical day look like? What does she love or hate about her job? Would she be willing for you to shadow her for an hour or a day?

After you've collected data through conversations and hands-on experience, take a closer look at whatever life option felt the most aligned with your Original Medicine, most free and expansive to your body, and most coherent with your Life Mission Statement. Rate the three options and choose one of them for the next exercise. You can run all of them through the next exercise but start with the one that feels the most exciting first.

Working Your Timeline Backward

This is a brilliant technique I learned from Barbara Sher. The process involves planning backwards from your goal. Most of us believe that because action goes forward, planning must too, which is not true. Planning backwards eliminates these common pitfalls:

- Starting out by taking the wrong steps
- Not being able to see how you are ever going to get anywhere and ultimately giving up
- Taking steps in the wrong order

For example, if you are planning to open a business, you might find the perfect location for the business and sign a lease before securing the finances to be able to pay the rent.

Creating a backward timeline chunks down what seems intimidating into small doable steps that can be accomplished one by one.

Your Backward Flowchart

This is a visual framework for brainstorming. When complete, you will have a detailed map of the pathway to get from the present moment to your goal. Your flow chart will be a visual map that guides you through the different phases of your plan.

Create a backward flowchart for each of your three alternative lives. Starting with the one that most excites you.

1. On a large piece of paper
    a. On the left side write today's date
    b. On the right side write the title of the alternative life version.
    c. Put down the date (even if it's hypothetical) when you will be complete with creating this alternative life.

2. What needs to happen right before the life version is complete? Then before that?

3. Work your way all the way back to today.

Add Dates to Your Flowchart

Now, you'll add dates to each step of the flowchart. Estimate how long each step will take, working forwards from today. It's okay if you need to adjust the completion date of your project.

Taking Small Steps

When facing your goal, after writing down what your universal self is yearning for, it's important to rest. Curl up in the fetal position. Rest is the critical first step to any important work. We must rest first to be able to create.

After resting, take a deep breath and chunk down what feels intimidating into smaller steps.

Great deeds are made up of small, steady actions, and it is these that you must learn to value and sustain.

– Barbara Sher

Ask yourself, "Can I complete this step tomorrow?" If the answer is no, break it down and determine what needs to be done first. The steps, at least at the beginning, should be so ridiculously small, it would be absurd not to do them. Keep breaking steps down into smaller components until you find a mini-step that you're sure you can accomplish easily. Take the one step that's right in front of you. Keep taking one more step. Heroes walk their scary paths one shaky, trembling step at a time.

During the process, pay close attention to your body's inner guidance. You will feel a positive shift in your body when the steps have become small enough.

Today, take one small step toward your goal. Just one. Then STOP! Don't take another step until you feel a strong desire to move on. At that point, take one more, small step. Then stop again, and so on. This strategy though it may seem slow, will make gradual, steady and sure progress. Along the way, question limiting beliefs as they pop up, hold on to your thread, and keep that reptilian brain as calm as a cucumber.

Because our societal selves tend toward perfectionism, remember this: Done is better than perfect. Watch the path, not the obstacles and celebrate each step. Celebrating makes the process more joyful and it builds confidence. If you feel paralyzed in moving forward, are the steps you're taking small enough?

Lady's Mantle

Alchemilla vulgaris or Lady's Mantle, was highly

favored by alchemists who believed it to possess magical healing properties. The droplets of morning dew were collected from the soft, pleated, and cupped leaves.

Lady's Mantle has long been used in women's health for toning and bringing vitality to the female reproductive system. Plant medicine beneficially affects our physical as well as our emotional and spiritual bodies. Lady's Mantle inspires courage that helps us climb out of ruts, move forward from the past and become who we are supposed to be. What a perfect ally for staking your claim.

Alchemilla vulgaris,
Lady's Mantle

Our work is to get to the
point where we like ourselves,
not based on what other's think or say
about us, but because we genuinely accept ourselves.
This means not harshly judging our mistakes and failures.

Chapter 8:
THE UNIVERSE CONSPIRES

If you follow your bliss, you put yourself on a
kind of track that has been there all the while,
waiting for you, and the life you ought to be
living is the one you are living. When you can see
that, you begin to meet people who are in the field
of your bliss, and they open doors to you. Follow
your bliss and don't be afraid and doors will open
where you didn't know they were going to be.
— JOSEPH CAMPBELL

Right about now you might be thinking, "Who am I to create one of these fantasy lives? I'm not smart enough. I don't even have the education and training!" I ask you: Who are you to think you shouldn't? Creating your life's calling is your service to the world. The world needs your creative genius and not sharing it is selfish. If any of the greatest innovators in history like Leonardo Da Vinci, Marie Curie, Buddha, Thomas Edison, Georgia O'Keeffe, Jane Austen, or Susan B. Anthony had held back their genius and passion, it's clear how different our world would be. How devoid of light and beauty and freedom would life be if we didn't have their creativity and ingenuity? So, who are you to hold back yours? Don't get trapped in the belief that you must be perfect or nothing at all.

Yes, it's paralyzing and frightening to step into the risk of the unknown, to put ourselves out there and potentially fail and open ourselves to scrutiny, judgement and criticism. But we must. We need not do it alone though.

Women have always depended on community for sharing stories, being seen and heard, and deepening our identities as individuals within the context of the group. When we are part of the safety net of sisterhood, it becomes possible for us to be vulnerable—to expose our tender and wounded hearts so that they may be healed. This is how our vulnerabilities become strengths and how we can transform ourselves.

When we reveal the wounds within our souls and shed light and balm on each one, we contribute to life in our own unique and vulnerable way. This transforming of ourselves from within helps to transform the world. We contribute solutions to the issues of the world by solving the mysteries and often painful complexities of our own lives. To be known, to be wanted, and to be contributing, is essential for each of us. When we hold ourselves back because of self-induced shame, we are cutting off the lifeline of belonging.

Asking for Help

So many of us women don't know how to ask for help. We are so accustomed to carrying everyone else's burdens, we don't feel comfortable asking anyone to help us with ours. We can even refuse help when it's offered because we don't want to be perceived as not trying hard enough. The societal conditioning of the Good Girl. We do everything for ourselves but only after we finish doing everything for everyone else. Our work is to let go of being the saver and the fixer and learn how to ask for and receive help.

Allowing ourselves to feel the vulnerability of asking for help and support is crucial in disrupting this mindset. It can feel scary at first but like anything, it gets easier each time we ask for and receive help. And it builds our community, our tribe. Giving others the opportunity to help us builds relationships by providing them a way to share in our excitements, joys, frustrations, disappointments and triumphs. Helping each other is good for us, it makes us happier, healthier, connects us to others, and creates community.

When you finally get the nerve to ask for help, make your request as specific and direct as possible. Respect your friends enough to allow them to say "no." It isn't a rejection of you, they are only saying no to your request not your worthiness for love and belonging.

Mutual respect is built on being impeccable with our word and saying no when we need to, is essential for respecting ourselves and each other. Instead of hearing a friend telling us no as rejection, let's honor them for being clear about their boundaries. This is integrity in action.

Your Support System

We have established that you don't need to go it alone. And that you need to be brave enough to ask for help and get over needing to look like you don't need it. Because we do need help, we all do, and not asking for it is isolating. Everyone needs a support team.

You've gotten clear on what you want, and you have set a timeline with specific steps to achieve your goal. Think about who you need on your team. You might want someone who has experience or expertise in the topic. You might want someone who has done something similar. Make a list of all the resources you have available right now, your social circles, networking organizations, contacts from school, colleagues at work, people you see at the gym, and family members. Your support team should not only support you, but also teach, guide and cheer you on.

After you've created your list, next to each name, write how they might be able to assist you, whether it is by mentoring you on your business plan, answering questions about marketing, suggesting educational options, editing your blog post, helping you set up your website, or connecting you with someone in the industry who you could reach out to.

Find an accountability partner who will help you

stay on course and help you from sliding back or giving up. Your accountability partner should be someone who knows you well, understands what you want to do, is interested and excited about it, and will root for you as you pursue your goals. I suggest a quick weekly call to set goals with your partner. Make a timeline for the completion of the work you want to do, and report back as you complete the tasks you've committed to.

Bounce your ideas off your accountability partner. Ask her to listen and reflect back to you what they heard you say to get a better understanding of how your ideas sound to someone else. Ask her to point out blind spots she might have heard in your ideas, and to ask questions to guide you to those blind spots. Getting this objective viewpoint will allow you to see possibilities you hadn't considered.

Mastering Resilience Against Criticism and Rejection

When you start putting yourself out there on social media, through blogs, and as you build community through networking and asking for help, you may feel vulnerable. This is good, as this is how you will build courage. How often we believe everyone is scrutinizing our flaws. One of the many wonderful things I have learned as I've gotten older is something I've heard said: "When you're twenty, you're obsessed with what everyone is thinking about you; when you're forty, you stop caring what people are thinking about you; and when you're sixty, you realize that no one was ever thinking about you." Although our greatest fear is that someone will discover how flawed we really are, guess what? People aren't thinking about us as much as we think they are! They are consumed with their own fears. Don't let other peoples' thoughts, judgements, points of view derail you. Know the direction you want to take. Believe in the path ahead. Believe it so much that it doesn't matter what others think.

Our real enemies are not the people who judge us, but the judgements we inflict on ourselves. Criticism and rejection are part of life and the fear of them is worse than the reality. Don't let the fear of being criticized stop you from doing the work of your life. The more you practice putting yourself out there, you will build resilience over time. It's a lot like exercising a muscle, it gets stronger with repetition.

When you are critiqued or rejected (if you are asking for help and someone says "no" for example,) try not to mull it over and over in your mind giving it more energy than what it is. Watch the thoughts and the resulting feelings to the circumstance and try not to make criticism mean something more. Remember it only means that they disagree with your opinion, it's not about you as a human being. Evaluate the validity of the source because constructively and considerately offered feedback is helpful to our growth. Ultimately though, the most important opinion that matters is your own. Like my mom used to say: "You can please some of the people some of the time but you'll never please all of the people all of the time."

Visible and Invisible Help

Although help is something we believe we can do without, we are born needing help to learn and growth. Even as adults, we depend on others for our successes. As a writer, for example, I need you as a reader. We need different forms of help at different stages of our lives. As you embark on launching your life's work, you may need the practical help of a graphic designer or an accountant. What about invisible or unseen help, the divine grace that places us in the right place at the right time to cross paths with the exact person that will open a door for us?

Viktor Frankl, an Austrian neurologist and psychiatrist and Holocaust survivor, said, "Those who have a 'why' to live, can bear with almost any 'how'." Purpose is a self-organizing central life theme that guides how we prioritize the actions we take and how we impact the world. We want to know our lives have meaning and that we matter. Whether our Original Medicine is to inspire, teach, support, encourage, uplift, transform, create, the energy directs our goals and creates meaning and purpose. Life purpose is one of the greatest predictors of life satisfaction.

When we line up with our life purpose while at the same time creating the inner space to receive, synchronicities take place. Is it a miracle? Is it destiny? I don't know, but I do know that opening ourselves up, dissolving limiting beliefs, creating body awareness, and aligning with our purpose attracts invisible assistance.

David Whyte describes it so exquisitely in his piece *Help*: "Visible help is practical or transactional help, asking for visible help we ask for help with what we can see is troubling us or we pay for a bed and a meal on our onward way or we pay someone to work for us. But it may be that it is the second less easily recognizable and invisible help which is most crucial for stepping into the unknown. Though we can think of invisible help in the old sense of an intervention from angelic or parallel worlds, we can also think of it in an everyday, practical way: invisible help is the help that we do not as yet know we need. Invisible help is the help we are not quite ready for and all we can do is shape our identity toward revelation, toward being surprised, toward paying attention to what is just about to appear over the horizon of our understanding."

Trust in Universal Support

If you've ever sat in a park in the springtime and listened to the songs of the birds, the buzzing of the bees and breathed in the green grass and spring flowers, you understand how everything in the Universe is conspiring for our well-being.

Surrendering to the Universe necessitates not being attached to the outcome. We don't need to achieve our goal to be happy. When we *need* anything, we are dwelling in a sense of lack. This certainly gives the reptilian brain something to fret about! You've created a goal and a timeline to achieve it, but you don't NEED this outcome to be happy! Although creating your calling and your life's work fulfills the deepest potential of your Original Medicine, you don't need it for any reason other than that of being of service.

Connecting to your universal self is where the possibility for happiness dwells. Connecting and honoring the wise one within is where the deepest level of satisfaction can be found. Your center of peace nourishes lasting fulfillment, and this is what draws outward abundance.

Taking action towards your goal while at the same time, surrendering the outcome and trusting that it will all work out exactly as it should, is what co-creating looks like. The transformation of your inner state that you've been working on through practicing these exercises is how you will manifest a life calling that is aligned with your true nature. What we actively manifest is formed from our inner state of being.

You know what you want to create, this is the seed. You are fostering the inner state from your universal self, the soil, water, and light that represent the conditions for your creation to become a reality. Now you surrender it. Ask for what you want. "I want [this] with all my heart." This is your truth and there is nothing in your body or your psyche or your spirit that disagrees with that or feels out of integrity with it. Declare it and take responsibility for it and ask for assistance by saying

"This is what I desire! I am radically responsible for my reality and I could use a hand." You can ask for evidence, for signs and for proof that you are on the right track. If you are unclear of what it is you want to create, ask for guidance. "Make it obvious how you would like me to serve."

Take the pressure off yourself—remove that 75-pound burden off your chest. Put your desire in a box and hand it over to the Universe. If it is meant to happen, divine grace will make it happen.

Writing has been essential to my process of surrender. I feel deep gratitude for the morning journaling that lifts weight off my heart. I write the pain, anger, grief, and confusion out of my heart and in doing so surrender it to the Universe. Letting it go allows me to be present and find joy in the moments, knowing that I will be guided.

Releasing skepticism requires trusting that what you want is possible, and that you are worthy of receiving it. This trust demands that you release doubt, be aware of thoughts that are affecting your inner state and set aside worry and concern. I'm guessing you must be seeing why you did the prior work of preparing yourself. Now it's time to surrender, to trust and observe the synchronicities unfold like magic. One caveat, if you remain open to the benign forces of divine grace, you very well might attract something even better than what you could have imagined in your wildest dreams. There are no rules in dreaming.

During the five years after my father's death, I did

much of the work I have been guiding you through. As I reconnected with my universal self and formed a sense of my Original Medicine, I started having vivid colorful dreams about a three-year-old girl. In every dream, she had tossed blond curls, and she was wearing a white dress, her eyes full of light, her arms beckoning me. I dreamt of her most every night for almost nine months, somehow knowing that this was my future child.

On December 22, 1986, towards the end of this nine-month period, I made the spontaneous decision to go home to Maui and visit my mom and my sister. I called all the airlines (this was B.I.—before internet), and each customer service representative literally laughed at my request for a ticket from San Francisco to Maui the next day. On my last call, to Continental Airlines, the lovely representative said, "No, I'm sorry we don't have any seats available for a flight from San Francisco to Honolulu (they hadn't opened direct mainland flights to Maui yet.) for the next two weeks. Oh wait! It looks like two seats just became available from Los Angeles to Honolulu. Would you like one of them?" So, I headed home the next morning via LA and Honolulu. You'll never guess who I ended up sitting next to on the plane. It was the future father of my daughter, the very being I had been dreaming about. Miracles do happen when we get out of fear and suffering and connect with the divine through our universal selves.

My journey has involved a series of struggles and awakenings that have brought me to an understanding of how this process works. I have seen nothing less than miracles happen when my clients have done this work.

Unhappiness and a lack of fulfillment don't mean that there is something wrong with you or that you haven't done enough. Develop a loyalty to the voice of your own guidance. As you do magic will begin to happen. Subtle and gentle, yet profound. You will feel comfort when you ask for it, guidance and support will show up in the form of teachers, dreams, and messages when you need them most.

> *The way back to my real environment, the place where my soul was meant to exist, doesn't lie through any set of codes I will ever find outside of myself. I must look inward. I must jettison every sorrow, every terror, every misconception, every lie that stands between my conscious mind and what I know in my heart to be true. Instead of clutching around me all the trappings of a "good" person, a "successful" person, or even a "righteous" person, I must be exactly what I am and take the horrible chance that I may be rejected for it. I can't get home by cloaking myself in the armor of any system, social, political, or religious. I have to strip off all that comforting armor and go on.*

> — Martha Beck

Chamomile

Chamomile is recognized as a relaxing nervine and is a common herb in sleep tea blends. As it relaxes our energy, it allows us to become receptive. When life feels challenging, it might be because you are resisting what you are being guided towards. Or you may not be receptive to the help and support that you need. Chamomile helps us let down our guard and let in the support and love of the Universe. Drinking a cup of delicious Chamomile infusion, relaxes and centers, providing a sense of well-being and support. It not only calms the body, it also relaxes the nerves and aids digestion. Chamomile is also wonderful for baths making it an ideal element of your self-care regime. Sit back, relax, breathe and receive.

Matricaria recutita, German Chamomile

"Within the seed of your desire is everything necessary for it to blossom to fulfillment. And Law of Attraction is the engine that does the work. Your work is just to give it a fertile growing place in order to expand."

— Abraham

Conclusion:
CONNECTING
THE DOTS

When it's over, I want to say: all my life I
was a bride married to amazement. I was the
bridegroom, taking the world into my arms.
When it is over, I don't want to wonder if I have
made of my life something and real. I don't want
to find myself sighing and frightened, or full of
argument. I don't want to end up simply having
visited this world.

— MARY OLIVER

This book is a guide to preparing your readiness for your calling and a life of purpose. The journey begins as you clear the path within yourself so that you can begin to see what you are meant for. As you connect into the magnificence of your divine self you will naturally begin to feel a connection to what you desire. Trusting in that inner wisdom will both inspire you to form your calling as well as attract it to you more quickly than you can imagine. Everything will start coming to you if you get to a place of peace. Follow your desire, not your fear.

We are meant for something more: a sacred life instilled with purpose. We are not here merely to survive each day and endure the pain. Beneath our conditioning lies a holy grail of divine possibility. A treasure chest of gifts and lessons that we must unearth and embody. Now is the time for each of us to bring all the creative energy that we are capable of giving to the nurture and healing of self, family, community, nation, culture and planet. We must mine the inspiration, creativity and knowledge from deep within our souls, the seat of our Original Medicine. It's time to come home to who you truly are.

We are never alone. We are all here for the same reason. To bring more love and light and kindness to each other. How we do that is unique to our own gifts, our Original Medicine. Opportunities show up every day to offer ourselves—whatever our job is, whatever our circumstances are right now, each moment of every day. But this does not happen in isolation or only when we are feeling successful. It happens whenever we choose to show up.

Create the work that brings you joy with certainty that life is happening for you and you are being supported in a way that every moment can be more wonderful than the moment before. Allow it in. Because you are worthy of success, prosperity and happiness. Go after it and lean into your accomplishments. Only you have your genius and your medicine. Offer it to the world. May your roots grow strong and deep and may your branches provide shelter during these uncertain times.

You are the one you've been waiting for.

The poet William Stafford's simple question: "Who are you really, wanderer?"

Blessings on your journey, fellow traveler.

> As human beings, we are as impermanent as everything else is. Every cell in the body is continuously changing. Thoughts and emotions rise and fall away unceasingly. When we're thinking that we're competent or that we're hopeless—what are we basing it on? On this fleeting moment? On yesterday's success or failure? We cling to a fixed idea of who we are, and it cripples us. Nothing and no one is fixed.
>
> —PEMA CHODRON

TRICIA ACHEATEL is an expert on women's empowerment, supporting women in their personal, professional, and entrepreneurial growth for over 27 years. She teaches women how to access their inner wisdom, develop self-confidence, and create with conviction—to shape a life of meaning. Her unique approach blends inner work with practical tools. She is a life coach, entrepreneur mentor, and medical herbalist and lives in Ashland, Oregon. You can find her at www.triciaacheatel.com

To access your free *Ideal Day Visualization* mp3,
after downloading the eBook, go to:
www.rootedinpurpose.com

I would love to hear about your experience with these principles, tools and exercises.
www.triciaacheatel.com/contact/

I'd be grateful for your book review on your online bookseller's website.

24153614R00111

Printed in Great Britain
by Amazon